DEMOCRACY
in the
American South

DEMOCRACY

in the

American South

Charles F. Cnudde
University of Wisconsin

MARKHAM PUBLISHING COMPANY
CHICAGO

Markham Series
in Empirical Democratic Theory
Deane E. Neubauer, Editor

BUDGE, *Agreement and the Stability of Democracy*
CNUDDE, *Democracy in the American South*

In memory of my brother,
Larry Cnudde (1947–1968)

Preface

This book began as my dissertation back in 1966. In the years since, I have added much that is new, different, and, in some cases, foreign to what I wrote then. In other cases I have made explicit some concepts and implications which were only implicit at that time. Perhaps the two threads that remain the same from then to now are my notions of how to conceptualize democracy and of how to relate contextual variables to individual behavior. In the latter I have been influenced by James W. Prothro and Donald R. Matthews through my graduate assistantship with their study which was published as *Negroes and the New Southern Politics*. The survey data that are reported in this book also come from their study.

I wish to thank them for these contributions to this book and for reading earlier drafts of it. I also wish to thank William R. Keech, Alden Lind, and Deane E. Neubauer for their comments. My wife, Susan Cnudde, typed many versions of this book, made additional comments, and by her efforts, lessened my other responsibilities. I am more than grateful for her help. Miss Vickie Schachter also typed a portion of the manuscript and Robert Jackman served as my research assistant. Finally, special thanks go to Peggy Nenno of Markham for her editorial assistance.

C. F. C.

Madison, Wisconsin

Contents

CHAPTER ONE

Introduction

One fall in the latter half of the 1960's a freshman in a political science course at a great southern university argued that:

> If Congress makes states like Mississippi give Negroes the vote, it's undemocratic. The whites are the majority and they don't want to do it. If Congress makes them, it won't be letting the majority have its way. That's undemocratic.

This student was not alone in his confused concept of democracy, for many of his classmates quickly voiced their agreement. Moreover, the ability to twist the meaning of democracy is not limited to politically unsophisticated students. Candidates for high political office sometimes violate democratic ideals when it suits their electoral purposes. In the 1963 gubernatorial campaign the Mississippi Democratic party purchased newspaper space to advise voters to "Kill the two-party threat now! Keep Mississippi united and free!" [1] The purpose of the advertisement was to encourage a Democratic landslide in the November elections, since outstanding men had already been "selected" in the second Democratic primary. The appeal went on, "But a silk-stocking group, calling themselves 'Republicans' insist on annoying the people with another political campaign—a 'third primary.' " [2]

Factors such as equal suffrage, party competition, and general elections—which most Americans seem to feel are necessary to a democratic system—elicit ambiguous reactions among many south-

---

[1] *Tylertown Times,* October 17, 1963, p. 3.
[2] *Ibid.*

erners.[3] The problem here is, of course, the existence of the Negro. In order to maintain white supremacy, white southerners feel compelled to keep Negroes out of politics.[4] That this is undemocratic cannot be perceived by the white majority.[5] The emphasis on democracy in the general American belief system makes it necessary for white southerners to define democracy so as to encompass the political practices of the region.

This is not to say that all southerners are guilty of such thinking. Indeed, as Chapter Three points out, there has been a phenomenal growth in political equality in many areas of the South. The Civil Rights efforts of the mid-1960's brought large increases in black political participation; however, some areas had made strides toward equal suffrage even before that time. Over the years between 1900 and the early 1960's, large numbers of blacks were added to the voting rolls in many communities.

AN APPROACH TO STUDYING DEMOCRACY

These developments present an interesting case of a "natural experiment" in the growth of this aspect of democracy. If we can explain why democracy developed in certain areas while it did not in other areas of the South, we can begin to make inferences about democratic development in general. If the processes which gave rise to democracy over this period can be pinned down, the research in the area of democratic theory will move another step forward.

The reason for examining democracy in the American South is therefore not so much because of an intrinsic interest in the politics of that section, although the political patterns there are among the most interesting in the nation, but because of theoretical

---

[3] In general, the weakest adherence to specific democratic processes among the regions of the United States is to be found in the South. See Samuel A. Stouffer, *Communism, Conformity, and Civil Liberties* (Garden City, N.Y.: Doubleday, 1955), pp. 129–130.

[4] For the overwhelming effect of the Negro presence on white politics in the South see V. O. Key, Jr., *Southern Politics* (New York: Vintage Books, 1949).

[5] More recent Congressional debates over voting rights may have decreased misperceptions here. A forthcoming study of the southern poor by Lewis Lipsitz and David Tabb may shed light on this possibility.

reasons. The South is the test case for this research because among the communities and states of the region we can find easily observed differences in democratic practices. From these differences we want to be able to make inferences about change in democracy.

It may seem strange to say so, but this emphasis on change is not altogether common in the research on democracy. Much of this research proceeds from hypotheses and assumptions of the importance of "consensus" on democratic values.[6] It sets the "maintenance" of democratic rules of the game and "democratic stability" as the outcomes that need explanation. These foci seem to be derived from, or at least are consistent with, integration theories. In these theories the emphasis is upon the interconnectedness of social relationships and a resulting equilibrium of such relationships once interrelationships have been established. For this reason, the viewpoint most prominent in integration theory is one which leads the researcher to analyze stability rather than change.

On the other hand, the approach adopted in this book comes closer to what are often called "conflict" theories.[7] In these theories the focus is upon those social elements that are out of equilibrium with other elements; therefore, it is upon situations of less interconnectedness, of strain and change. Of course, these two viewpoints, conflict and consensus, are not completely in opposition to one another; rather, they are two sides of the same coin. Therefore, these distinctions cannot be overdrawn; it would be improper to choose a research example and describe it as completely within the consensus school with no elements of, or recognition of, conflict in political relations. Yet tendencies to lie somewhat more toward one of these positions than the other do seem to exist. These tendencies, in turn, lead scholars to ask somewhat different questions of the same phenomena and to look at somewhat different parts of the world for answers.

In much of the previous research, perhaps because of the theoretical approach adopted, the observations of democracy, as

---

[6] For a summary of this literature see Charles F. Cnudde, "Elite-Mass Relationships and Democratic Rules of the Game," *American Behavioral Scientist* (forthcoming).

[7] See Ralf Dahrendorf, *Class and Class Conflict in Industrial Society* (Stanford, Calif.: Stanford University Press, 1959), and Pierre van den Berghe, "Dialectic and Functionalism: Toward a Theoretical Synthesis," *American Sociological Review*, 28 (1963), 695–705.

we will see later in this and the next chapter, are constants rather than variables. For some purposes, as in discussions of the prerequisites of democratic stability, this kind of observation may be appropriate. In order to add to our knowledge about democracy information concerning what factors change the level of democracy in a political system—making it more democratic in some cases, less in others—we must proceed with some approximations of change in this characteristic. With a view to making inferences about change in democratic practices, we will look at the differences in such practices that exist in the United States. As we will argue in Chapter Three, these differences are most apparent and easy to measure in the South. In that chapter and in Chapters Four and Five we will test hypotheses about which variables explain the differences that exist in the region.

The adoption of an approach that focuses upon change does more than point to the South as a crucial area for this investigation. It also leads to a recognition of the inadequacy of several previous definitions of democracy. Sometimes democracy has been equated with the practices observed in a particular political system. An emphasis on change, however, requires a conception that can vary less or *more* than the practice that exists in a particular time and place. As a result, the next chapter will discuss concepts of democracy and will present an alternative which, theoretically, can vary beyond the level of democracy that exists in any "real" political system.

Similarly, the emphasis on change leads to less reliance upon consensus on democratic values than upon the *degree* of agreement to democratic values. It should be obvious by now that the former tends to be associated with stability and the latter with change. Finally, the approach heightens the visibility of the normative context as a possible influence on behavior. Since change can be generated from either internal stress or from the need to adapt to external forces, the conceptual distinction between internal and external forces is an element in change theory. Because the approach makes one aware of this conceptual distinction, a likely hypothesis for investigation is that an individual may be motivated not only by his own values but also by the values of those in his normative context: in his immediate community, state, regional, or national environments.

Many of the tests in this book, then, are of the impact of the context within which individuals live upon their behavior—especially upon behavior that relates to democratic practices. The contextual hypothesis in these tests attempts to relate what are normally called aggregate variables to other variables measured at the individual level. Specifically, variables reported for counties—obtained from the United States Census—will be interrelated with variables reported for individuals—obtained from survey research. This type of methodology is becoming quite common as a way to get additional "mileage" out of both types of data sources. In addition, the contextual hypothesis also leads to tests which involve aggregating additional variables from the survey responses. In this case, the individual responses are converted to a proportion of those who respond one way or another in the geographical unit used as the basis of the sampling clusters in the survey, the Primary Sampling Units. Since these P.S.U.'s are normally counties or metropolitan areas the context can normally be viewed as a community.

In a sense, then, the approach used in this book leads to both new ways of defining concepts and of making hypotheses about their interrelationships. These, in turn, lead to a methodology that gives operational indicators appropriate to tests of the hypotheses.

CITIZEN ATTITUDES AND DEMOCRATIC PRACTICES

Essentially what this book is about is whether or not citizen attitudes toward democracy, treated as an aspect of the normative context, have any relationship with the practice of democracy within that context. Two sets of previous theorizing are relevant to this concern; one predicts no relationship between the two variables, the other predicts some relationship. The hope is to integrate these studies or to choose between them. The first series of studies, which concerns the importance of mass consensus on democratic values, was referred to earlier in this chapter. The conclusion that consensus is not a precondition for democratic procedures has often led to the further interpretation that there is no relationship between mass attitudes and political procedures; that we should look to elite values as the explanation for existing procedures. The arguments from the consensus literature will be developed more fully in later chapters.

The second group of hypotheses concerns a more detailed

analysis of the role of the rules of the game. It would lead us to expect some relationship between these variables. It holds that the existing rules of the game are rarely questioned by most citizens; that their existence is taken for granted.[8] Because of this, alternative procedures are not taken seriously, and are dismissed out of hand. In this sense we might expect some relationship between citizen attitudes and the existing rules of the game.

This second field of theorizing has serious shortcomings because it generally leads to predictions about non-observables or about non-occurrences.[9] For this reason it is necessary to examine more thoroughly the implications of the hypothesis in this chapter.

As the first step in doing so, it is necessary to point out that a further bias, or assumption, of this book is that it views political equality as an important aspect of democracy. The study will attempt to provide at least partial explanations of the variation in a measure of this factor in the South. Furthermore, the view of democracy taken here is that it is a characteristic of political practices or "rules of the political game." Yet since the rules of the game are, by definition, the overarching practices that structure the nature of political activity, we are rarely in a position to measure variation in them. That is to say that within any political regime these rules are more or less constant. Therefore, it is difficult to test hypotheses about the factors which relate to these rules.

Nevertheless, the rules of the game may have a great deal to do with how and what political decisions are made and, therefore, with the distribution of power. Thus:

> . . . power is exercised when A participates in the making of decisions that affect B. But power is also exercised when A devotes his energies to creating or reinforcing social and political values and institutional practices that limit the scope of the political process to public consideration of only those issues which are comparatively innocuous to A. To the extent that A

---

[8] See E. E. Schattschneider, *The Semisovereign People* (New York: Holt, Rinehart, and Winston, 1960), and Peter Bachrach and Morton S. Baratz, "The Two Faces of Power," *American Political Science Review,* LVII (December 1962), 947–952.

[9] Richard M. Merelman, "On the Neo-Elitist Critique of Community Power," *American Political Science Review,* LXII (June 1968), 451–460.

succeeds in doing this, B is prevented, for all practical purposes, from bringing to the fore any issues that might in their resolution be seriously detrimental to A's set of preferences.[10]

For example, in restricting our analysis to observable decisions, we often may not capture situations in which the really important matters are excluded from political decision. In this "wider political sense," the existing rules of the game may remove all subject matter from consideration except that which is trivial to a certain group's interests.

Yet in what sense is this a theoretical possibility if it cannot be observed? If the change in the dependent variable relevant to the hypothesis cannot be observed, then isn't the hypothesis a tautology that can never be disproven? I think the distinction here is not one between rejectable and nonrejectable hypotheses, but between experimental versus nonexperimental research.

The empirical research on power and influence has been almost entirely non-experimental. That is to say, we wait for decisions to occur naturally, and then attempt to ascertain what influences account for them. There are many chances for erroneous inferences in nonexperimental research. One of the more obvious ones is simply that the range of behaviors that is available in natural settings may be simply too limited to test adequately some kinds of hypotheses. In such cases, these hypotheses remain as theoretical alternatives, and the inability to test them in natural settings does not constitute grounds for rejection.

As opposed to examining whatever dependent behavior happens to occur, the procedure in experimental design is to test hypotheses by introducing treatments hypothesized to cause certain dependent behaviors, and by then examining whether or not the behaviors in fact occurred. Specifically, to experiment in this case requires that demands be made from groups that are presently without influence because they have preferences for alternatives excluded by the rules of the game. If these demands are defeated due to the activation of individuals and groups with greater influence, then the hypothesis is not rejected.

Thus the required test is the experimental activation of new demands that threaten to change the whole definition of permissible

---

[10] Bachrach and Baratz, "Two Faces," p. 948.

political discussion. The response predicted by the hypothesis is a defeat of this set of demands as a result of the anticipation of reactions of additional individuals and groups, or by the counter activation of these individuals and groups. In this manner, observations can be made on an overt decision even if it is a remaking of the decision in favor of the status quo.

Yet scholars will rarely have the opportunity to conduct experiments aimed at providing answers to questions of this sort. Therefore, the fallback strategy of exploiting opportunities for employing quasi-experimental designs will normally have to be utilized.

An obvious way to use such quasi-experimental approximations is to be on the lookout for situations that pose challenges to the existing institutionalized practices. That is, if the dominant values structure political activity, then the only test of whether this is so is the occasional deviant case that represents a threat to the existing practices. The appropriate test cases, then, are those issue demands that occur from time to time which are so contrary to decision-makers' expectations that they represent changes in the usual terms of political discourse.

To this end, we will have to be sensitive to the naturally occurring "mobilization" of previously quiescent groups such as the poor, blacks, students, etc. These groups have often made demands upon local governmental agencies with which they had previously had little direct contact. These demands have often been for major innovations in the rules of the game—innovations such as the inclusion of new groups in decision-making functions. The frequency of such events in recent years means that social scientists have had many opportunities to investigate the hypothesis of unconscious influence in nonexperimental analyses.

Another deviant case to be discussed in Chapter Three is the practice of many Southern communities with respect to Negro registration. Whereas the restrictions on the right to vote are cumbersome in many states, we have little reason to believe that they exist to intentionally increase the power of the franchised remainder. In the South, however, this was clearly the intention of those restrictions which discriminated against the registration of Negroes and, in some cases, poor whites as well. Moreover, our assumptions about this practice are that the reason for these restrictions is the desire to prevent the changes in public policy which

Negro participation would lead to. That is to say, equality in the voting booth might lead to attempts to increase the extent of social equality via the enactment of local and state legislation outlawing racial segregation.

Therefore, the disenfranchisement of the Negro can be interpreted as a structuring of the rules of the game in order to prevent certain policy alternatives from being considered. Although it is quite possible that the rules of the game often place constraints on which options are available in policy-making, the evidence needed to test this hypothesis is hard to come by. The South, however, contains these practices relative to the Negro which, since they are so blatantly discriminatory; make it relatively easy to observe the variables in the hypothesis. At the same time, the South today is being bombarded with mass communications originating outside the region. We therefore can expect some individuals to consider the distinction between southern political practices and the meaning of democracy in the wider culture. We may find some greater conflict and questioning of the rules of the game than is usual. This means that the findings here may or may not be generalizable to other situations. But the deviant case of these features of the South does make it possible to have at least some type of nonexperimental test of a hypothesis that is otherwise untestable. As a result, we can at least see if the hypothesis has any validity at all.

Conclusions

Translating the hypothesis about the role of the rules of the game into more precise social science language, we can say that the rules of the game are a set of dependent variables which are supported by the norms of important sectors of the population. These rules, in turn, restrict the policy alternatives available, of course. So in principle the set of variables also serves as independent variables which relate to other types of policy outcomes that are chosen. In this study, this relationship will be a defining characteristic of the rules of the game. If procedures are not intended to so restrict policy outcomes, they are not included in our set of dependent variables. The entire discussion of the role of Negro registration in social science analyses leaves little question that it fits this definition.

The question under study, however, is whether or not the

variation in this procedure can be said to be supported by the norms of sectors of the population. Therefore, the types of independent variables under investigation are the attitudes and opinions of citizens. The inferences that are under question are whether or not the rules of the game vary, and if everything else is equal, whether or not they vary when the values of citizens vary.

If the answer to the question seems to be in the affirmative, then it seems reasonable to say:

1. There is some evidence for the hypothesis that the rules of the game that restrict alternatives by ruling out demands by some groups are supported by citizen norms.

2. Therefore, there often may be some relationship between citizen values and the rules of the game, even if citizen values rarely reach a consensus on such procedures.

A final assumption made in this book is that democracy refers to some actual behavior or occurrence. To explain democracy is, therefore, to explain certain operative features of political systems. It may sound trite to say these things about the nature of democracy; but, surprisingly enough, even well-informed political observers use the term in excessively legalistic ways. For example, when speaking of democracy in America we often refer to the Constitutional guarantees contained in the Bill of Rights. Yet when we remember that institutionalized social processes are produced by norms, mores, *and* laws, it is clear that the reference to the law alone does not give us the necessary and sufficient conditions for the existence of democracy. In the chapter that follows, a concept of democracy will be developed which, unlike the conception of the student at the beginning of this chapter, will make use of the ancient ideal version of the word; but which will also lead us to focus upon the actual political processes of systems and not merely "the law."

CHAPTER TWO

Political Democracy
and Empirical Theory:
Conceptualization and Hypotheses

The idea in the consensus literature that democratic practices in a political system are possible if there is a consensus on democracy, may or may not be subject to empirical test.[1] If we assume that it is, it requires, first of all, that consensus and democracy somehow be treated as two variables to be interrelated, or at least as two clusters of variables. Moreover, it requires that we conceive of democracy as something to be explained, and that what the population thinks is one of the things that explains it. The assumption underlying this statement is that democracy is the dependent variable and the attitudes of the citizenry are the independent variables; that the former is the effect and the latter the causes.

In this chapter these two concepts will be treated as variables. Some of the issues surrounding that treatment will be made explicit. Hopefully, this procedure will prevent misconceptions such as that of the Southern undergraduate of the introductory chapter. If so, we can proceed with the task of examining empirical explanations of democracy.

THE CONCEPT OF DEMOCRACY

Before turning to an explanation of democratic patterns in the South, we must attempt to complete the crucial and long overdue

---

[1] See the discussion of the traditional thinking on consensus in James W. Prothro and Charles M. Grigg, "Fundamental Principles of

task of setting out a clear definition of democracy. Several problems loom large in this attempt. In the early stages of the development of a science a high proportion of its vocabulary is likely to be made up of terms of customary usage; consequently, the meaning of these terms is apt to be too vague for extensive scientific development. At some point in the development of a science, a more precise vocabulary is necessary for the continued growth of the science.

The social sciences, as immature scientific disciplines, employ many terms that are vague in their meanings. *Democracy* is a term that causes peculiar difficulties in social science analysis. It has a long history of usage in the intellectual development of the Western world, having had different connotations at different times in history. Since the term is much older than the social sciences as we now know them, it has meanings which exist irrespective of the needs of scientific precision. At the same time, however, the term as it has been defined until now has been very useful to political scientists, having been used to make efficient discriminations between types of political systems. As a result, there appears to be a beginning of an empirical theory of democracy in which certain patterns of social relations regularly give rise to political democracy and other patterns seem to be effects of democracy.[2]

Therefore, although there are major problems in using the term in empirical research, the basic concept seems to have importance and utility. Further attempts should be made to clarify and refine current usage, rather than turning to purely nominalist definitions for comparisons of political systems. Such clarification would result in a definition of democracy that has greater utility for empirical social science and, at the same time, retains much of the "meat" of the customary use of the term.[3]

Democracy: Bases of Agreement and Disagreement," *Journal of Politics,* XXII (1960), 276–294.

[2] An empirical study of this nature is Seymour Martin Lipset, "Some Social Requisites of Democracy: Economic Development and Political Legitimacy," *American Political Science Review,* LIII (March 1959), 69–105.

[3] For the procedures of scientific definition see Carl G. Hempel, "Fundamentals of Concept Formation in Empirical Science," *International Encyclopedia of Unified Science,* II, No. 7 (Chicago: University of Chicago Press, 1952).

Explication of terms is a difficult process because it proposes a precise definition for ideas which are usually held to be intuitively clear to most people. The danger is always present that the explication will be charged with having failed to meet someone's intuitive understanding. Accepting the possibility of such charges, this chapter sets out the following program as one of its goals:

> Taking its departure from the customary meanings of the terms, explication aims at reducing the limitations, ambiguities, and inconsistencies of their ordinary usage by propounding a reinterpretation intended to enhance the clarity and precision of their meanings as well as their ability to function in hypotheses and theories with explanatory and predictive force.[4]

The first step in explicating democracy is to point out some issues that will override the main effort. First of all, the view of democracy discussed is a qualified one. We are considering political democracy rather than democracy in general, which would include social and economic democracy as well.[5] If we consider these as separate concepts, their interrelationships become a matter of empirical test rather than assumption. This strategy appears to be more efficient and convenient than the alternative. The qualification, however, means that only political behaviors are under consideration. Statements of the effects of these behaviors, such as those usually included in Madisonian and Marxian democracy, are excluded from the immediate discussion. These other uses of the term have extensive economic and social content. In Madisonian democracy, restrictions on democracy are instituted to protect the social and economic positions of the upper strata; in Marxian democracy these positions—and strata—are eliminated. If democracy is seen as a type of purely political behavior, these conflicting alternative results become hypothetical rather than definitional.

Another aspect of this effort at definition is that it is conceptual and not operational. Therefore, "real world" problems of measure-

---

[4] *Ibid.*, p. 12.

[5] Ranney and Kendall discuss some of the literature that takes the opposite point of view. However, they themselves seem to agree with a qualified definition of democracy. Austin Ranney and Willmoore Kendall, *Democracy and the American Party System* (New York: Harcourt, Brace & World, 1956), pp. 12–13.

ment are being ignored momentarily. Concepts will be viewed as interval scales on which political systems vary in degrees even though few available measurements are so precise. This strategy is taken because it aids theoretical clarity to be able to consider causal relationships between variables that have such precise characteristics. Also, the definition of democracy eventually explicated will be conceived of as one dimension, even though several alternative operational dimensions can be used to measure it.

The fact that this effort at definition is conceptual implies a third, more general, qualification. In order to serve their functions in science most effectively, concepts are defined in variable terms; that is, observations are thought of as having more or less of the attribute being defined. At their most precise level, factors in science are conceived of as varying according to degrees. Even though we often intuitively feel that one nation is more democratic than another, the usual definitions of democracy preclude such rankings because they are not unidimensional. They therefore are not characterized by the parsimony necessary for even this degree of precision. The goal of this explication will be to develop a conceptualization of democracy which can better serve the function of a variable in scientific hypotheses and, at the same time, retain most of the conventional meaning of the term.

With these issues in mind, we will turn to the previous uses of the concept of democracy. An attempt will be made to sort out the logic of these definitions and to remove redundancies in order to arrive at the most economic statement of their meaning. First a discussion of the historical use of democracy will be considered and then the more contemporary political science usages will be explored.

HISTORICAL MEANINGS OF DEMOCRACY

Ranney and Kendall evaluate much of the historical usage of the term. Their analysis indicates three areas of consensus among traditional scholars on what is essential to the meaning of the word. Democracy must include political equality, "the right of each citizen to count as one in the decision-making process"; governmental response to the popular will, "government should do whatever the people want it to do and should not do anything they object to"; and majority rule, "if the government has the legitimate power in any given matter to act at all . . . it should do whatever the majority of the members of the community want it to do." [6] In a later section, the authors go on to develop four principles of democracy. These are popular sovereignty, political equality, popular consultation, and majority rule.[7]

It appears that two of these principles—popular consultation and popular sovereignty—are closely related to governmental response to the popular will. Popular consultation requires three conditions:

> (1) on matters of public policy there must be a genuine popular will;
> (2) the officeholders must be aware of what that will requires; and
> (3) having ascertained the nature of the popular will, they must then faithfully and invariably translate it into action.[8]

Popular consultation, therefore, is a mechanism for keeping the government responsive to the popular will, since it specifies officeholder's behavior as following the popular will. Governmental response to the popular will is thus a more general requirement which will be fulfilled if the specific mechanism of popular consultation is followed.

Moreover, taking another step back in levels of generality, popular sovereignty seems to be a general principle from which governmental responsiveness is derived. The authors indicate that "the doctrine of 'popular sovereignty' then, is that according to which power vests in all the members of the community rather than in any part of them or in any one of them." [9] If power is vested in the members of the community, then the government of the community should be responsive to the popular will, that is, it should do what the people want it to do and not do what they don't want it to do.

When there is popular consensus on policy proposals, popular

---

[6] *Ibid.*, pp. 16–17.
[7] *Ibid.*, p. 23.
[8] *Ibid.*, p. 28.
[9] *Ibid.*, p. 24.

sovereignty can follow in a straightforward manner. The government simply does what the populace wants. If the government doesn't, then it isn't democratic. But what should the government do when there is no policy consensus? If the people are divided, the government surely should not refrain from any action. If a proposal happened to be an innovation in policy, then doing nothing would, in effect, be deciding in favor of those who were against the innovation. In the absence of action, one of the disagreeing groups gets its way. Therefore, it is logically impossible for the government not to decide in favor of one group or the other once a policy becomes a matter of popular consideration. There are no grounds for saying that the group opposed to innovation represents the popular will any more than another group.

Since the government makes a policy decision in any case, on what grounds should it base its decision when there is policy dissensus? The doctrine of popular sovereignty offers no ideal solution to this problem. As long as the populace disagrees on policy, the political system cannot fulfill the absolute condition of popular sovereignty. Systems can tend to maximize this value to some degree or other, however. When there is disagreement, there is likely to be a majority and a minority position on the policy.[10] Because following the majority at least comes closer to the requirement of popular sovereignty than following the minority position, governments that follow majority rule are more democratic than those that do not, providing the other requirements for democracy have been met. Even when there is policy consensus, the majority principle does not conflict with the popular sovereignty requirement. Then the majority will be one of 100 percent. If political systems follow the spirit of the majority principle, they will achieve or best maximize popular sovereignty.

Observation of political systems in the world indicates that policy disagreements very often exist. Therefore, the majority principle is a common, or perhaps even the most general, method of approximating popular sovereignty. Majority rule, moreover, is

---

[10] When the populace is split fifty-fifty, the requirement of popular sovereignty is undefined except by "governmental indifference or deadlock." See Robert A. Dahl, *A Preface to Democratic Theory* (Chicago: University of Chicago Press, 1956), p. 39.

at an even more technical level than the other concepts implied in democracy. This rule is a procedure, almost at the operating level, which democratic systems follow. Thus the concepts of popular sovereignty, governmental responsiveness to the popular will, popular consultation, and majority rule—from the point of view of the existence of democracy—seem to be increasingly more specific conditions for fulfilling the same requirement. Popular sovereignty will be maximized if there is governmental responsiveness to the popular will. Government responsiveness will be maximized if there is popular consultation. Popular consultation will be maximized if there is majority rule. Thus, to determine how democratic a political system is (as long as the requirement of political equality has been met) it is not necessary to compare it to other systems on all four concepts, but only on the most general one, popular sovereignty. It is only when we want to design institutions to facilitate democracy that it is necessary to consider the more specific procedures for democracy. When we want to measure democracy, however, we can simply conceptualize systems on a dimension of popular sovereignty because these other dimensions are merely procedures for maximizing it.

Of course, on the operational level it is difficult to compare political systems on popular sovereignty because this term is so general. However, here we are concerned only with the most parsimonious conceptual definition of democracy. Therefore, the generality of the term is an asset rather than a liability.

This discussion indicates that there are two primary criteria, the fulfillment of which determines whether or not political systems are democratic or not democratic. These criteria are popular sovereignty and political equality. The former concept stands for several others suggested by Ranney and Kendall's discussion of the historical usage of democracy; the latter is also suggested by these authors although it has not yet been fully evaluated. This chapter will now turn to the contemporary political science usage of both of these terms. It will restrict the discussion, however, to studies using behavioral definitions of democracy, rather than to those which analyze democratic character, democratic personality, or democratic attitudes. This will be done because, for the purposes of this study, democracy will be treated theoretically on a system level rather than on an individual level.

POPULAR SOVEREIGNTY AND
POLITICAL EQUALITY

In the decades following World War II, many American political scientists became convinced that democracy referred to something concerning the actual practice of political systems. Before that time, perhaps because much political science was then addressed to the study of Western governments, democracy was seen as involving aspects of the legal structure of government. However, Westerners observe that developing nations governed by military dictatorships often have constitutions that are consistent with most scholars' ideals of what democracy means. In a sense, then, concentration on political practice as the view of democracy has made this topic a subject of "behavioral" inquiry within political science.

Even in more recent political science work, there are weaknesses in definitions of democracy. Because of difficulties encountered in research, democracy is often defined as popular sovereignty. When democracy is not the central object of a study, the definition of the term may be haphazard. In studies of political parties, for example, party competition is said to be necessary for democracy.[11] It is apparent that only one aspect of democracy, popular sovereignty, is being used as the definition here. Some competition between political parties seems to be necessary in order for popular choice, and therefore, for popular sovereignty, to exist. One problem with viewing democracy as popular sovereignty is that another aspect of democracy, the political equality of all citizens, does not necessarily follow from popular choice. During times of crisis, parties may advocate and threaten the destruction of the rights of political minorities. Historical examples of this are the rise of authoritarian parties in pre-war Europe and the McCarthy movement in the United States in the 1950's.

Moreover, this possibility is partially what normative theorists mean when they speak of the basic tension between popular sover-

---

[11] The early writings that take this position are summarized in Austin Ranney, *The Doctrine of Responsible Party Government* (Urbana, Ill.: University of Illinois Press, 1962), pp. 25–110. See also Ranney and Kendall, *Democracy and Party System,* and V. O. Key, Jr., *Politics, Parties and Pressure Groups* (New York: Thomas Y. Crowell, 1958), pp. 7–20.

eignty and minority rights.[12] In a democracy, as we have seen, policy decisions are apt to be made by some procedure following the principle of majority rule. It is therefore always possible for the majority to decide to eliminate the rights of a certain political minority. Since this possibility exists both theoretically and historically, it cannot be said that party competition is necessary for achieving democracy, but only for approximating popular sovereignty.

A second problem involved in viewing democracy as popular sovereignty is that the latter is undefined when the populace is equally divided over alternative policies. This problem is related to, and is probably a special case of, the problem of cyclical majority.[13] Thus, mathematically speaking, majority rule may break down if three or more individuals rank order three or more policy alternatives.[14] Out of every possible pair of alternatives, each alternative may be preferred over the others by a majority. Unless the construction of pairs is being manipulated, the result will be deadlock. Riker indicates that the likelihood of the cyclical majority problem increases with ". . . the lower the degree of consensus in the decision-making body, whether it be a committee or a nation." [15] This problem, therefore, is more likely to occur when the populace is equally divided over the alternatives.

If the construction of pairs is manipulated, then the result is minority rule. This is clearly undemocratic, since it is another violation of political equality. The members of the minority who decide between the alternatives have more political influence than the members of the majority. To the degree that this occurs, the political system exhibits a degree of political inequality.

---

[12] For this effect of party, see Ranney, *Party Government,* pp. 113–147.

[13] Of the writers on this problem, Riker and Dahl have considered it most directly in terms of its implications for empirical democratic theory. See William H. Riker, "Arrow's Theorem and Some Examples of the Paradox of Voting," in S. Sidney Ulmer, Harold Guetzkow, William H. Riker, and Donald E. Stokes, eds., *Mathematical Applications in Political Science* ("Arnold Foundation Monographs," Vol. XII; Dallas: The Arnold Foundation, 1965), pp. 41–60, and Dahl, *Preface,* pp. 39–43.

[14] For a proof of this that is illustrated with political examples, see Riker, "Arrow's Theorem," pp. 43–52.

[15] *Ibid.,* p. 60.

On the other hand, without manipulation the result is deadlock. Empirically, deadlock normally means the maintenance of the status quo. Since the populace is equally divided over the alternatives, the status quo alternative is preferred by less than a majority. Thus, deadlock also results in political inequality.

Majority rule, the operating technique most consistent with the requirement of popular sovereignty, therefore can conflict with political equality in specific instances. Therefore, on several grounds, this requirement is not a sufficient definition of democracy.

Another difficulty in research, the problem of measurement in cross-national research, also may lead to less than satisfactory definitions of democracy. Thus the empirical proposition that party competition is highly correlated with democracy is less restrictive than the statement that party competition is necessary for democracy. Since the maximization of popular sovereignty is implied in party competition, and since democratic political systems operate in part under the doctrine of popular sovereignty, most cases are likely to have party competition and democracy simultaneously. Therefore, occurrences such as Nazism in Germany and the McCarthy movement of the 1950's are only deviant cases. Because of this kind of thinking, party competition is often used as a rough conceptual indicator for democracy, either because a scholar is hesitant to define democracy itself, or because he knows that few operational measures of democracy are available.

Lipset utilizes this kind of conceptualization in his cross-national work on democracy. He defines political democracy as:

> . . . a political system which supplies regular constitutional opportunities for changing the governing officials. It is a social mechanism for the resolution of the problem of societal decision-making among conflicting interest groups which permits the largest to choose among alternative contenders for political office.[16]

In another cross-national study of democracy, Phillips Cutright uses a similar definition of the concept.[17] Indeed, in a second-

---

[16] Lipset, "Social Requisites," p. 71.

[17] Phillips Cutright, "National Political Development," in Nelson W. Polsby, Robert A. Dentler, and Paul A. Smith, eds., *Politics and Social Life* (Boston: Houghton Mifflin, 1963), pp. 569–582.

ary analysis of Cutright's data, McCrone and Cnudde find evidence that increases one's willingness to think in these terms.[18] Using factors relating to party competition as a dependent variable, the authors show that it is possible to infer a causal model that is consistent with much of the important theorizing about democracy contained in the political development literature.

There are two difficulties with these views of democracy. First, although most scholars are probably willing to agree that party competition and democracy are highly correlated, it is an assumption rarely tested; instead, the one variable is used as an indicator for the other. Second, even if the assumption were tested and found to be correct, the correlation between the two variables would undoubtedly be less than perfect. To the extent that they were imperfectly correlated, the variables would be imperfect indicators for each other. Therefore, even though the studies mentioned have been important in the development of this field, further progress requires that there be a better definition of the concept and fewer untested assumptions.

The conceptual definitions of Dahl and of Prothro and Grigg are very similar and are the most intuitively satisfying of those to be found in the literature to date.[19] Of the two, Dahl's definition is more extensively worked out. Like Prothro and Grigg, he postulates two conditions necessary for democracy. Thus:

> An organization is democratic if and only if the process of arriving at governmental policy is compatible with the condition of popular sovereignty and the condition of political equality.[20]

Therefore, both popular sovereignty and political equality must exist before democracy can be said to exist. The primitive terms that define these two conditions are:

> The condition of popular sovereignty is satisfied if and only if it is the case that whenever policy choices are

---

[18] Donald J. McCrone and Charles F. Cnudde, "Toward a Communications Theory of Democratic Political Development: A Causal Model," *American Political Science Review*, LXI (March, 1967), 72–79.

[19] See Dahl, *Preface,* and Prothro and Grigg, "Principles of Democracy."

[20] Dahl, *Preface,* p. 37.

perceived to exist, the alternative selected and enforced as governmental policy is the alternative most preferred by the members.[21]

and:

The condition of political equality is satisfied if and only if control over governmental decisions is so shared that, whenever policy alternatives are perceived to exist, in the choice of the alternative to be enforced as government policy, the preference of each member is assigned an equal value.[22]

Democracy is, therefore, a governmental practice such that the policies instituted are those most preferred by the members of society when the members' preferences have equal weight. Although this satisfies intuitive notions that democracy implies something about political equality and citizen participation in policy-making, it is restrictive on other grounds. Consideration of Figure 2-1 will make this clear.

Figure 2-1 is a graphic representation of Dahl's definition; it indicates that democracy is present only when two conditions are met. The problem here is one that is common in many definitions current in political science. Whenever an attribute is defined in terms of two other concepts occurring jointly, it is impossible to think of the attribute as varying by degrees.[23] Within the framework of Figure 2-1, democracy cannot occur more or less or by degrees across political systems; instead, according to the logic of

---

[21] *Ibid.*

[22] *Ibid.*

[23] In other words, it is difficult to think of concepts so defined as mathematical functions of other variables, that is, as their causes or effects. Hempel says that scientific definitions of concepts that do have this nature cannot be defined by genus and differentia. Figure 2-1 shows that democracy has been defined in this way. Democracies are there defined as the intersection of the class of popular sovereignty-type systems and the class of political equality-type systems. See Hempel, "Concept Formation," pp. 4–5. Of course we could imagine applying some equivalent of vector algebra to this type of problem. However, then we would have to decide on the relative weight of political equality and popular sovereignty in the measure of democracy. There are no theoretical grounds for making such decisions. Moreover, as will become apparent below, there is a simpler solution to the problem.

the definition, it is either present or absent, depending on whether popular sovereignty and political equality are present or absent.

If we define democracy as an either-or proposition, then we unnecessarily limit our ability to theorize about the causes of it. We cannot hypothesize that some other factor increases or decreases democracy, but only that it tends to make democracy present or absent. A more satisfactory view is that democracy theoretically varies by degrees; this conceptualization lends itself better to building causal theories. It explicitly calls for hypotheses that specify variables that produce changes in the degree of democracy in political systems.

		Popular Sovereignty	
		Yes	No
Political Equality	Yes	Democracy	Non-democracy
	No	Non-democracy	Non-democracy

Figure 2-1. A Typology of Democracy According to the Conditions of Popular Sovereignty and Political Equality

Moreover, this view is not only a more rigorous scientific employment of the term "democracy," it is also more consistent with informal, common sense usages. We normally think that some nations are *more* democratic than others. If a state disfranchises 20 percent of its potential electorate, we think that it is less democratic (everything else being equal) than one which disqualifies only felons and the mentally deficient. Another hypothetical state that enfranchises just 50 percent of its potential electorate would generally seem less democratic than either. Thus our formal definitions make democracy an either-or characteristic, while our informal usages make it a more-or-less variable. This ironic state of affairs indicates that further explication of the term is necessary.

One possible way out of this dilemma is to argue that the two underlying requirements—popular sovereignty and political equality—vary by degrees themselves, rather than being present or absent. As a result, democracy varies according to the scores on the underlying dimensions. This is a revision of the above definition, yet it still may not be completely satisfactory for many scientific purposes. Unless we are willing to assume that the underlying variables are perfectly correlated, the possibility exists that one political system may have a higher score on popular sovereignty than it does on political equality. Also, another system may have a lower score on popular sovereignty than it does on political equality. When this occurs, it is impossible to ascertain which system is more democratic. Democracy, then, is a partially ordered scale.[24] In spite of the fact that such scales are more precise than those implied in the original definition, they are far from the unidimensional concepts necessary for building the most precise causal theories.

A similar alternative argument may be that democracy is an ideal and, as such, is one extreme end of a spectrum of democracy. Since no specific political system can meet an ideal, the political systems can be placed along the spectrum according to the degree to which they approach the ideal. This argument seems to be compatible with the idea that democracy is a matter of degree. It does not, however. Implied in this argument is the presence of two other ideals—popular sovereignty and political equality—which political systems may approach by degrees. It is thus the location of a political system on the latter two spectra which determines its place on the spectrum of democracy. Again, unless popular sovereignty and political equality can be conceptualized as perfectly correlated, political systems can have higher scores on one of these spectra than they do on the other. This strategy also achieves a partially ordered scale and its associated difficulties.

The only solution to these problems is to draw conceptual cutting points on the spectra of popular sovereignty and political equality, qualifying as democratic those systems that are over the

---

[24] It is perhaps instructive to note that Coombs implicitly assumes that researchers rely on variables that are conceptually unidimensional, and that partially ordered scales arise primarily because of problems in measurement. Clyde H. Coombs, "Theory and Methods of Social Measurement," in Leon Festinger and Daniel Katz, eds., *Research Methods in the Behavioral Sciences* (New York: Holt, Rinehart and Winston, 1953), pp. 474–475.

cutting points on each spectra, and qualifying as undemocratic all other systems. This is exactly where this discussion started and is what is implied by Figure 2-1.

These problems could be by-passed, if the assumption could be made that the two underlying spectra are perfectly correlated. If, however, they were perfectly correlated, both spectra would not be needed in the definition. For operational purposes, democracy could then be defined in terms of only one of them, since it would also imply the other. A solution similar to this one, which, how-ever, does not assume perfect correlation but, relying instead upon the internal logic of these definitions, will be utilized in the defini-tion of democracy proposed in this chapter.

Before defining democracy as it is used in the present study, a necessary qualifying remark must be made concerning the fore-going discussion. The problems cited above are involved in con-ceptualizations of democracy for the purposes of empirical research; their importance for purely normative political thought is, at the most, minor. For example, in normative discussions it may be help-ful to define terms as absolute values rather than as attributes that vary by degrees. Under such conditions, the definition of democracy analyzed in Figure 2-1 presents no problems. It is per-fectly consistent with the purposes of normative thought, then, to define democracy as an ideal that occurs when two other ideals occur. Also, it is sometimes helpful in normative thinking to con-sider only one aspect of democracy—such as majority rule. This may be true if the value of primary interest has been shown to be derived from that one aspect of democracy. Although it is loose thinking, then, to use only one aspect of the concept as the defini-tion of the concept, it can be done in this case without serious error.

However, when concepts are employed in empirical theory, additional problems, as has been shown, ensue. Ideally, concepts in empirical theory must serve at least two functions. They must contain all that scholars mean by the idea, and they must, at least theoretically, be conceived of as unidimensional attributes that vary by degrees. In the case of defining democracy these two re-quirements are in conflict. The most commonly accepted idea of democracy includes two conditions, popular sovereignty and polit-ical equality; defining in terms of two conditions makes it difficult to think of the concept as varying by degrees. In order to make further advances in the empirical study of democracy, this dilemma must be overcome. To do this, we must explicate Dahl's conceptions somewhat further.

Dahl derives a proposition from his definitions of popular sovereignty and political equality which states that "the only rule compatible with decision-making in a populistic democracy is the majority principle." [25] In stating this proposition, Dahl is primarily concerned with popular sovereignty: he is giving meaning to the phrase "the alternative most preferred by the members." His proof shows, however, that political equality is also necessary to the proposition.[26] Thus the only interpretation of "most preferred" that is consistent with equally weighted preferences is "preferred by the majority." If we follow Dahl in being willing to let popular sovereignty mean majority rule, then, in a certain sense, when we say "political equality" we are also saying "popular sovereignty."

This development requires closer examination. The term political equality as it is used by democratic theorists means equality in sharing control over governmental decision.[27] Political equality therefore has popular participation in governmental decision-making built into its definition. Moreover, Dahl has shown that only under majority rule can political equality be maximized.[28] Therefore, while majority rule can exist without political equality, political equality logically implies popular sovereignty or—operationally speaking—majority rule. Therefore, political systems arrayed over a dimension of political equality will be assigned the same position on a dimension of democracy as on the dimension of political equality. This is true because majority rule is utilized in the definition of political equality. Both conditions necessary

---

[25] Dahl, *Preface,* p. 37.

[26] For Dahl's proof see *ibid.,* pp. 60–61.

[27] Ranney and Kendall also take this position: "Thus political equality means not only 'one man, one vote,' but also an equal chance for each member of the community to participate in the total decision-making process of the community." Ranney and Kendall, *Democracy and Party System,* p. 28.

[28] This is a necessary part of Dahl's proof. Dahl, *Preface,* pp. 60–61. Ranney and Kendall concur: "There is, we believe, no logical alternative to majority rule except minority rule; and of the two, majority rule must be chosen as a principle of democracy, since it is more nearly consistent than minority rule with the other principles of democracy." *Ibid.,* p. 34.

for democracy are met if one of them, political equality, is met. This explication depends upon the logic of usual usages of these terms.

Letting popular sovereignty equal majority rule does not upset common uses of these terms. The preceding discussion indicates that many scholars have even equated majority rule with democracy. Consideration of their work shows that they were in fact talking about one aspect of democracy, popular sovereignty, when they made the equation. Therefore, Dahl's usage, which is being relied upon here, has fairly common currency.

Yet, it is the meaning of political equality that is central to the view of democracy being developed here. If the meaning of the term, political equality, has not included popular participation, then redefining the term to include it is merely an exercise in semantics which would obscure rather than clarify the necessary conditions for democracy. That this is not the case can readily be seen in the logic of the term. If political equality does not refer to participation in governmental policy choices, then political equality has little to do with democracy. In the Soviet Union, for example, each citizen has an equal vote in national elections; however, voting has little to do with governmental decisions. Leadership selection and policy-making take place among an extremely small group of party and government officials. Consequently, Westerners would accord the USSR a very low place on a scale of political equality, and thus, democracy. If, on the other hand, the leaders of the Soviet Union decided to make sure that the preferences of every citizen counted equally in making policy choices, which basis would they institute for making choices when agreement was not unanimous? Majority rule is the only such basis; anything less than majority rule would mean that the preferences of some citizens had greater weights than others. When political equality is maximized, so is majority rule.

THE SCIENTIFIC OBSERVATION
OF DEMOCRACY

Since the requirements for democracy are maximized when political equality is maximized, only the latter need be observed to measure the degree of democracy in political systems. It would be redundant to measure popular sovereignty or any of its derivatives also. With only one requirement being needed to measure democracy, the term can be conceptually defined as a matter of degree rather than as either present or absent in political systems. Thus democracy is a varying attribute of political systems which depends upon the extent to which those systems approach absolute equality among members' preferences as the basis for political decision-making. This type of definition facilitates the use of democracy as a variable in causal hypotheses. It therefore brings a higher degree of precision to our thinking about the concept.

Under this definition no existing political system qualifies as perfectly democratic. This results from the use of the conventional definitions of democracy as the core of our explication; those definitions postulated absolute requirements for the existence of democracy. Any empirical political system must necessarily be conceptualized as a deviation from the absolute. That these deviations can be conceptualized as occurring by degrees is the innovation suggested by this study, since it postulates a unidimensional requirement, political equality, for democracy's existence.

The definition of political equality used here is the usual one and, as such, is an ideal that represents one end of a spectrum. The location of political systems on the spectrum can be conceived of as the extent to which they fulfill the condition of political equality, that is, the degree to which they approach the ideal. However, the location of a political system on a dimension of popular sovereignty is not the same as its location on a dimension of political equality. In mathematical terminology, the two dimensions necessary for democracy are asymmetrically related (see Figure 2-2).

Figure 2-2 indicates that all political systems that fulfill the condition of political equality also fulfill the condition of popular sovereignty, as is shown by the cross-hatchings. However, not all systems that fulfill the condition of popular sovereignty also fulfill the condition of political equality. This is shown by the vertical lines on the outer rim of the figure. Therefore—although the majority can decide to limit political equality by destroying the rights of political minorities—as long as political equality is maximized, political decisions, by definition, can be made only by maximizing the majority principle.

This point has been missed by many democratic thinkers,

probably because they were primarily concerned with the problem of majority tyranny. The normative interests of most early writers led them to be crucially aware of the fact that the majority in a democracy is always able to restrict the political rights of some minority, that is, to minimize political equality. That such an act is undemocratic probably would not trouble majorities today, say contemporary writers, because of the low adherence of citizens to

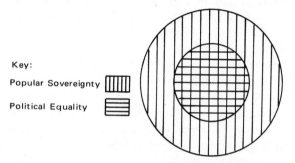

Key:

Popular Sovereignty

Political Equality

Figure 2-2. The Asymmetrical Logical Relationship Between the Two Conditions Necessary for Political Democracy

democratic values.[29] Therefore, much thinking about democracy centers on the power of the majority and on attempts to limit that power in order to maintain political equality. Such problems make it clear that it is not enough to define democratic political systems as those in which the majority rules, but as those in which the political equality of minorities is also maintained.

As has been shown, this history of thinking about democracy has hampered empirical research in the area. In empirical analysis the immediate goal is not so much to protect or to maintain democracy as it is to measure it. Efforts at measurement ideally require conceptual definitions that involve one underlying dimension per concept, in order to avoid the difficulties already pointed out. In the case of democracy, the concept can be defined so that it can be measured by the dimension of political equality.

---

[29] For contemporary data, see Samuel A. Stouffer, *Communism, Conformity, and Civil Liberties* (Garden City, N.Y.: Doubleday, 1955); Prothro and Grigg, "Principles of Democracy"; and McClosky, "Consensus and Ideology in American Politics," *American Political Science Review*, LVIII, 361–382.

That this view of democracy solves empirical and not normative problems should again be pointed out. Empirical relationships can test assumptions of fact contained in normative systems. Therefore, definitions of variables that are testable can contribute to value theory by making possible tests of their empirical relationships. However, efforts at purely definitional clarity by empirical scholars usually have only limited importance for normative thinkers. More specifically, the normative problem remains that where political equality exists today, it—and therefore democracy—may not exist tomorrow. Precision in definition can only clarify, not do away with, that problem.

However, by examining the logical meaning of the several conditions thought to be necessary for democracy, we can conclude that, for the purposes of empirical analysis, only one of these is of central concern. If a researcher is interested in how democratic political systems are at one point in time or how they vary on democracy over time, then the extent to which they approximate the requirement of political equality is what he should observe. If he gains that information he will have gained what is essential to measurements of democracy.

Since an adequate conceptualization of democracy can be reduced to one dimension, the term can be used more rigorously in scientific hypotheses. In viewing variation in democracy as variation in fulfilling political equality, scholars can examine the kinds of public policies that are likely to be produced by degrees of democracy. Also, the concept can be used as a dependent variable so that other variables can be related to it to explain the variation in democracy in political systems. This study will attempt to do this in the case of the South.

In order to explain the existence of varying degrees of democracy in the eleven former Confederate states, an attempt will be made to measure degrees of political equality in the region. This measurement will serve as the dependent variable of the study. Testing in order to determine which independent variables might help explain this variable requires that a set of hypotheses first be constructed. The next section will postulate a general hypothesis in light of the literature in political science concerning proximate factors that have been found to be important in explaining democracy.

A CONTEXTUAL THEORY
OF DEMOCRACY

Not only does the concept of democracy developed here enable us to treat it in variable terms, it also contains hints at a cluster of hypotheses that may help to explain the variable. In positing a variable notion of democracy, this concept anchors the upper level of the variable in an ideal—an ideal similar in nature to the concept of a vacuum in physics. That this ideal may never be reached does not hamper its conceptual use for fixing the central content of the definition, but it does sensitize us to the possibility that there exist "real" conditions that limit the achievement of the ideal. Hypothesizing what some of these conditions may be, then, becomes an exercise in theory-building about the causes of democracy—causes that, in some cases, go beyond those hypothesized in the literature, and that, in other cases, reinterpret previous findings.

What this book proposes to investigate is a contextual hypothesis concerning democracy. If democracy is the varying degrees to which political behavior approximates complete political equality, then we cannot explain such approximations without knowing the normative context within which the behavior is imbedded. The less complete our knowledge of the context, the less complete our explanations. For example, many analyses of democracy refer to its legal aspects, such as guarantees against governmental interference in rights to participate, or to characteristics of other political structures, such as competition between political parties. Yet even if such factors were completely maximized, the ideal level of democracy probably would not be reached. The reason for this lies in the social context in which political behavior takes place.

One of the consequences of the fact that men live together in social groups is a certain amount of conformity to group norms. The explanations for conformity may range from individual needs to the necessary functions of groups to historical accident. Whatever the reasons for conformity, its impact is to dampen the potential for individual choice—upon which the ideal conception of democracy was based. Even if the laws say that I can speak freely on political issues, the mores of my community may make it impossible for me to take certain positions. In that case, I do not have complete equality with my neighbor who speaks freely because he happens to agree with the prevailing view. The fact of human society, therefore, makes it nearly impossible to achieve complete democracy.

A qualification of the status quo implications of this thinking must be made. Although the contextual hypothesis partakes of Sumner's social theory, we can, like Myrdal, guard against Sumner's "do-nothing" valuations.[30] If one wishes to maximize democracy, then the strategy is to seize upon the deviant cases (that is, those individuals who do not conform to community values and those groups that tolerate dissent), investigate the conditions under which those cases occur, and attempt to maximize those conditions.

Nevertheless, it may be impossible to design a political system that has complete political equality; this only means that no system will meet the absolute end of the continuum. We can imagine such possibilities, just as we can imagine a vacuum or absolute zero in order to lay the conceptual foundations for scientific measurement of those variables. Thus, if we are interested in measuring democracy rather than writing democratic constitutions, we do not need to limit ourselves to "realistic" conceptions of it.

From an empirical point of view the explicit recognition of the possibility of deviant cases raises the notion of *variation* within the proportion of the population that conforms to standards of either democracy or its opposite. If there is variation among communities to the extent to which there is agreement to some important value, then that variation could include both *conflict* and *consensus* on the value. One extreme would contain communities in which there is a consensus in favor of the value; at the midpoint, communities in which there is complete *conflict* on the value; and the other extreme, communities in which there is consensus against the value. In addition, there may be a range of communities that fall elsewhere among these points. The research strategy adopted here is to try to determine the impact of the whole range of com-

---

[30] For an excellent discussion of Sumner's theory, see Gunnar Myrdal, *An American Dilemma* (New York: McGraw-Hill, 1964), Appendix 2.

munity agreement—rather than merely consensus—on democratic values.

The central hypothesis that leaps forward from these statements is that the twin ideas of varying agreement to democratic values as a community context and varying levels of democratic practice in the community may go hand in hand. This means that, despite previous research, we hypothesize that agreement to democratic norms may be an important determinant of democracy. This does not mean that previous research is wrong, but that it may be reinterpreted in light of the developments in this chapter. In short, the following review will show that the previous literature deals only with a special case of the contextual hypothesis.

Prothro and Grigg's initial investigations opened this field to empirical research by finding the previously held assumptions of popular democratic consensus to be faulty.[31] Up to that time, scholarly thinking usually took the form of imputing mass consensus on democratic rules of the game as a causal factor of democratic practices.[32] Prothro and Grigg's findings provided a basis for rejecting mass consensus as an explanatory variable, therefore making necessary a search for other possible explanations for democratic systems.

V. O. Key's analysis of American public opinion led him to make inferences about the functions of the political leadership in maintaining democratic practices. He concludes:

> The norms of the practices of politics in an order that has regard for public opinion include broad rules of etiquette governing relations among the activists, as well as rules governing the relations of activists with the public. . . . All these elements of the rules of the game gain strength, not from their statement in the statutes and

---

[31] Prothro and Grigg, "Principles of Democracy."

[32] This assumption still can be found creeping into the literature. Thus, "In general, this management of cleavage is accomplished by subordinating conflicts on the political level to some higher, overreaching attitudes of solidarity, whether these attitudes be the norms associated with the 'rules of the game' or the belief that there exists within the society a supraparty solidarity based on non-partisan criteria." Almond and Verba, *The Civic Culture* (Princeton, N.J.: Princeton University Press, 1963), p. 492.

codes, but from their incorporation into the norms that guide the behavior of the political activists.[33]

Key would seem to hypothesize, then, that the values of the leadership should be looked to for an explanation of democratic patterns.

Dahl's reflections also point to this higher political stratum as the source of democratic stability.[34] Dahl expects that, in New Haven, and even elsewhere in the United States, the same minority of the population that possess the highest levels of political interest, skills, and resources also possess a high degree of adherence to democratic norms. The majority, on the other hand, may not agree to these values, but lack the skills and interest to employ their comparatively meager resources efficiently. Because of a positive association between democratic norms and political stratification, democratic rules of the game exist despite the lack of mass consensus on those rules.

McClosky's findings tended to confirm hypotheses that move activist consensus to the fore as the major alternative explanation. He found that a comparison of individuals who differ even a small amount on a political stratification dimension resulted in different levels of agreement to democratic rules of the game.[35] Party convention delegates hold much higher degrees of agreement to these norms than the general populace in the United States. Preliminary inferences changing the originally assumed proposition to incorporate the empirical findings of Prothro and Grigg and McClosky might be put thus: An explanation of democratic practices in political systems is the high degree of activist agreement to values respecting those practices in those systems in the absence of mass agreement, or when combined with mass disagreement, acquiescence, or apathy.

A more detailed examination of this body of research makes it clear that three concepts have been basic to these inquiries. First, the dependent variable is democracy. Thus, these findings are based upon research conducted in the United States with the explicit assumption that the United States is a highly democratic political

---

[33] V. O. Key, Jr., *Public Opinion and American Democracy* (New York: Knopf, 1961), p. 539.

[34] Dahl, *Who Governs?* (New Haven, Conn.: Yale University Press, 1961), p. 315.

[35] McClosky, "Consensus and Ideology."

system. The examination of patterns of consensus is therefore a search for explanations for this dependent variable.

The other concepts employed are popular and elite consensus on democratic values. Given a three variable system with a specified dependent variable, a variety of logical interrelationships are possible. Following McClosky, the possibility that all three concepts are independent of each other can be rejected. Similarly McClosky and Prothro and Grigg indicate that one relationship cannot be rejected, that between elite consensus and democratic practices; and that one can be rejected, that between popular consensus and the dependent variable. Figure 2-3 represents diagrammatically the prevalent thinking in this area.

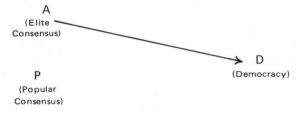

Figure 2-3. Relationships Between Elite and Popular Consensus on Democratic Norms, and Degree of Democracy Suggested by Research to Date

Despite the amount of thinking and research devoted to these issues, none of the relationships in this model have been adequately tested for our purposes. All of the studies referred to above utilize democratic practices at the national level in the United States as the dependent variable. Key, Stouffer and McClosky deal only with national data and observations. Authors who deal with case studies below the national level attempt to generalize beyond those cases: Prothro and Grigg make little mention of the differences between Ann Arbor and Tallahassee. Rather, they are concerned with the existence of democracy nationally, despite a lack of consensus on democratic values not only in the two towns, but, by extension, in the country as a whole. Dahl discusses explicitly the nature of democracy in New Haven, but he just as explicitly states that he doubts that New Haven differs markedly from the rest of the country in that respect.

Because the studies have been theoretically or operationally studies of the nation, they have been analyses of one case. As in all studies with an "N" of one, what we normally think of as the independent and dependent variables have not been variables at all, but have been constants. To take McClosky's study just as an example, we find elite agreement approaching a consensus on democratic values and, at the same time, we find a certain amount of democracy in the United States. However, we do not know what conditions of activist agreement would be associated with different levels of democracy, because varying levels of democracy have not been measured. We would need to have this information to support the inference that the level of democracy is due to activist attitudes or values.

Moreover, since the level of democracy at the national level remains essentially constant throughout the time period of any one study, the concept of democracy, to a large extent, has been identified with the political practices in America. In other words, there has been a confusion of operational and conceptual definitions such that the operational definition of most studies, the American practice, has been utilized to redefine the concept. The rationale for doing so has been to achieve a more "realistic" definition of democracy. By that, I think, is meant a level of democracy that is attainable by real political systems. Sartori has pointed out the normative difficulties that this kind of thinking entails.[36] In addition, this "realistic" redefinition causes scientific difficulties that could be avoided. By identifying democracy with what exists in one nation at essentially one point in time, we make it difficult to think about change in the level of democratic practice. So, in essence, the impact of our realistic definitions has been to make hypothesis-building about democratic change extremely difficult and, correspondingly, to foreshorten the theoretical growth of this area of empirical analysis.

Similarly, the concern with consensus on democratic norms as the independent variable in the model developed thus far also limits those measures—if not to constants—at least to attributes of very limited variability. Thus agreement may or may not reach the level of consensus. Once again we have a dichotomous variable. On the other hand, the reconceptualization in this chapter specifies

---

[36] Giovanni Sartori, *Democratic Theory* (New York: Praeger, 1965).

varying degrees of conformity to community values concerning democracy. Therefore, even though the level of democracy practiced in the United States does not require mass consensus, the level of democracy may still be conditioned by the level of agreement to those norms.

In short, the previous findings on consensus do not address themselves completely to the present question. Those findings may still stand and still we may find that agreement to democratic norms is related to the level of democracy. The reason for the lack of contradiction is the difference in the variables; on the one hand we have constants and dichotomous variables and, on the other, factors that differ by degrees.

In this chapter a new definition of democracy has been presented, a definition that makes it possible to think of democracy as a continuous variable. The conception is the varying approximation of an ideal, complete political equality. The retention of the ideal as the grounding of the content of the definition sensitizes us to the importance of non-governmental factors that may produce variation in democratic practices. Thus the entire normative context in which behavior takes place—the mores, values, as well as the laws—becomes an important predictor for democracy. In the following chapters, then, we will examine the impact of the nature of the community upon democratic practices.

CHAPTER THREE

Democracy in the South: The Social Setting

One of the main arguments in the last chapter held that the surrounding normative context places constraints upon how closely human behavior approximates the democratic ideal. If this theory is correct, we would expect that empirical measures of the local context would be related to measures of democracy. The present chapter will make some preliminary tests of these relationships after operationalizing the concepts in the theory. In addition, as a central part of the operationalizing process, some speculations will be offered on some possible impacts of the wider context— that is, the impact of the *national* and *regional* settings which are necessarily unmeasured in a study of purely *local* effects.

Theories and empirical tests have a different logical status. Theories are made up of propositions that are not specific to time or place; Tests of theories are carried out, however, with data from the "real" (observable) world and are therefore based on specific temporal and geographic cases. Although this dilemma is an unavoidable one, its disconcerting effects can at least be recognized by examining the characteristics that might be peculiar to the case chosen as the test site.

Since the South in the 1960's has been chosen as the test site for this study, we will examine the social setting peculiar to that region. In so doing, we will operationally define the measure of democracy that will serve as the dependent variable of the study. Thus, although the previous chapter set out the reasons for viewing political equality as an adequate scientific conceptualization of democracy, there are many alternative ways to operationalize this dimension. In the best of all possible worlds, studies of representative democracy would attempt to measure such complex factors as citizen participation in defining policy alternatives; malapportionment at all levels of government; and corruption at electoral, legislative, judicial, and executive levels, as well as restrictions on citizen participation at all levels. Hopefully such studies will be undertaken and, eventually, an index of political equality will be constructed which will combine these and other indicators. Until then, the most efficient research strategy would seem to be one which seizes upon the most crucial indicator of political equality in the historical context of the case under research. A brief review of the southern setting will attempt to show that the registration of Negroes, as the main focus of controversy over democracy in the region, is the crucial indicator for this study.

This chapter will also consider several operational definitions of the social setting of the region. The test of the contextual hypothesis set out in the preceding chapter requires that we do so. Thus the selection of Negro registration as the dependent variable means that the relevant context for this measure of democracy is the nature of the surrounding, dominant white society. This context will be related to Negro registration in three ways. First, a brief discussion of the history and the nature of the southern region will demonstrate the utility of the choices made in operationalizing the latter variable. Second, this chapter will sort through a group of indicators for the differences among the local communities in the South—indicators that may serve as important contexts for the participation of Negroes in those localities. Third, the remaining chapters will use additional contextual variables to interpret and thereby spell out further the theoretical implications of any contextual relationships discovered.

DEMOCRACY AND THE RIGHT TO VOTE

In the United States, state and local governments have the legal responsibility to administer elections for offices at all levels in the federal system. The act of casting one's ballot in elections is a political activity at the mass level—one over which these institutions of government have much control. Other forms of mass political activity are more informal and not so subject to governmental scrutiny. Citizens can engage in political discussions with their neighbors and even go to rallies and campaign meetings without coming into contact with the legal machinery of government. Even less public types of political behavior, such as making campaign contributions, can often be engaged in despite the opposition of the political system.[1] The only way that these informal modes of activity can be restricted by government is through police state actions. Short of police state conditions, undemocratic activity by formal government agencies often centers on restricting a certain political minority's right to vote.

Although, ideologically, the right to vote may be a "right" of American citizens, legally it must be earned by fulfilling certain requirements. These range from proof of residence to proof of literacy and, until recently, payment of a tax.[2] The burden of proof that these requirements have been fulfilled is placed upon the citizen. The point at which the citizen comes before the governmental authority to show that he has met the requirements for voting (when he registers to vote) is the point in this process at which political institutions can exert the greatest amount of control.

Thus requirements for registering to vote can be affixed so as to have a differential impact among various groups in the population. For example, if the majority wishes to exclude a political minority from making demands on the political system, and that minority has a common social background in which educational achievement is minimal, then literacy requirements for making demands will effectively bring about political inequality. In the American South, there is evidence that even the application

---

[1] Matthews and Prothro, for example, find that under conditions of political discrimination we can find repressed groups making "scalar errors" in the normal sequence of increasingly difficult forms of political behavior. Thus southern Negroes who may be prevented from voting by the political system can make secret campaign contributions, usually a more difficult kind of activity. Donald R. Matthews and James W. Prothro, *Negroes and the New Southern Politics* (New York: Harcourt Brace & World, 1966), Chap. 2.

[2] For a description of registration requirements in the South and their effects on southern whites, see V. O. Key, Jr., *Southern Politics* (New York: Vintage Books, 1949), pp. 555–643. For the effect of these and other factors on southern Negroes, see Donald R. Matthews and James W. Prothro, "Political Factors and Negro Voter Registration in the South," *American Political Science Review*, LVII (1963), 355–367.

of these tests in the registration process was carried out in a way discriminatory to Negroes, perhaps because many poor whites in the region were also comparatively uneducated.[3] The differential impact of discriminatory legal requirements is thereby enhanced by discriminatory enforcement.

Such political inequalities could be achieved at a time when widespread restrictions on the freedom of speech and other authoritarian methods would be more difficult to implement. An important point here is that many of the legal restrictions on registration can be argued in terms other than those of liberal democracy. The democratic man model, with its emphasis on the informed and active citizen, can be used to support literacy tests and to placing the burden of proof on the citizen.[4] Political inequality may exist with respect to registration of voters even in a society which has a public ideology of democracy.

Although a complete test of the democratic nature of political systems would include a broad range of measures on political inequalities, the foregoing comments suggest that restrictions on the registration of the Negro are a manifestation of undemocratic practices in the South. Voting is an important mass-level political activity. The power to deny registration for voting is easily manipulated. Under conditions of a public democratic ideology, differential registration of voters can be defended more easily than other forms of political inequality. For these reasons, the nonregistration of Negroes in the eleven former states of the Confederacy will be utilized as an indicator of infringement on the rights of the political minority.

The existence of the Negro Political Participation study, with the largest sample of Negro adults yet drawn from the South,

---

[3] Gunnar Myrdal, *An American Dilemma* (New York: McGraw-Hill, 1964), pp. 483–485.

[4] While this "rationality-activist model" is considered a dead horse among social scientists, it seems to survive as a functional myth at the mass level. See Gabriel A. Almond and Sidney Verba, *The Civic Culture* (Princeton, N.J.: Princeton University Press, 1963), pp. 481–487; and V. O. Key, Jr., *Public Opinion and American Democracy* (New York: Knopf, 1961), p. 547. Although this model often is ascribed to normative theorists, the classical literature has little to say on the subject. See William R. Keech, "Classical Democratic Theory and the Classical Democratic Citizen" (Master's thesis, Department of Political Science, University of Wisconsin, 1962).

facilitates operationalizing concepts such as minority rights.[5] Rather than relying on the intuitive notions of informants or participant observers on how much political democracy exists in the South, a survey allows one to ask Negroes directly whether or not they are registered to vote. Answers to this question can be used to measure the extent to which minority political rights exist in the area of voting, which is an important dimension of democratic rules of the game. Affirmative answers of the Negro sample to the NPP study interview question, "Are you now registered in (county)?" will be taken to indicate the practice of democratic rules of the game on this dimension. Negative answers will be taken to indicate the lack of such practices. Contextual factors which explain the distribution of positive and negative answers to this dependent variable, therefore, will be conceptualized as explanations of this aspect of democracy.

In order to set the stage for the contemporary explanations of this variable, however, the historical place of Negro registration in the South must be examined. This examination will allow present rates of registration to be placed in perspective as part of an ongoing process of change over time in the politics of the region.

DEMOCRACY IN THE SOUTH

The denial of the vote to Negroes in the South has been a major undemocratic tendency within the United States. It is, therefore, a major dimension of democratic rules of the game on which significant variation can be measured within this country. Historically, there apparently has been some variation of this practice.[6] The destruction of the Reconstruction regimes did not immediately spell the end of political equality for Negroes. The Southern states vacillated on the issue of whether or not Negroes would be allowed to vote between the end of Reconstruction and the beginning of the Populist era. As late as 1896, over 130,000 Negro names were

---

[5] For a more extended report on this study, see Matthews and Prothro, *Negroes and the New Southern Politics.*

[6] The following discussion, unless otherwise noted, is based upon Paul Lewinson, *Race, Class and Party* (New York: Grosset & Dunlap, 1965).

on the registration lists in Louisiana.[7] Throughout this period Negroes were allowed to vote, as long as whites of all classes were monolithic in their support of conservative political parties. Under these conditions Negro voters were sometimes tolerated as members of the Republican minority and, at other times, were a manipulated conservative bloc marched to the polls by the plantation masters.[8] From time to time, however, whites split along economic lines and Negroes were appealed to as the deciding factor. Such appeals slightly increased Negro participation; but since these appeals threatened to upset Negro-white status relationships, such election campaigns were followed by a new white solidarity and by attempts to limit Negro participation.

The period from roughly 1876 to the early 1900's was one of political learning and innovation in the South. Political conflict among white social classes made southerners aware of the possible effects of free Negro political participation on the existing social structure. The desire to keep the Negro in a subservient position led to the creation of alternative techniques to limit Negro voting. The level of Negro voting seemed to fluctuate with the degree of white solidarity and with the disenfranchising techniques utilized.

In the 1880's and 1890's the Populist movement brought the clearest threat to white unity. Negro registration reached a high point at that time. The conservative Democratic party turned to racist appeals in order to reunite whites within the party.[9] The success of those appeals led to the enactment of the most effective restrictions on Negro participation developed since Reconstruction. A combination of locally administered literacy and character tests effectively eliminated Negroes from the registration lists; the vote of illiterate poor whites was protected under the "grandfather clause."

Thus the number of Negro names on the registration lists in Louisiana decreased 96 percent in the four-year period between 1896 and 1900. Comparative data on the other states are not available, although some indication of the meager number of regis-

---

[7] *Ibid.*, p. 214.

[8] On this point see Myrdal, *An American Dilemma*, p. 480.

[9] These appeals resulted not only in disenfranchisement for the southern Negro, but also in the wholesale enactment of "Jim Crow" laws. See C. Vann Woodward, *The Strange Career of Jim Crow* (New York: Galaxy Books, 1957), pp. 65–95.

tered Negroes in the post-Populist era is available. In Alabama, for example, less than 3.1 percent of the literate Negro males 21 years old and over were registered in 1908. In the most populous Negro county, of the 21,000 literate Negro males of age 21 and over, fewer than 400 were registered. In Hot Springs, Arkansas, only about 1,000 Negroes were registered at any time in the period from 1920 to 1930. In this same period there were from 200 to 500 Negroes registered in Atlanta; 50 to 100 in Jackson, Mississippi; 100 to 200 in Asheville, N.C.; 45 in Greenville, S.C.; 50 in Fayette County, Tennessee; 1,400 to 1,600 (about 10 percent of the literate, 21 years old and over, Negro population) in Dallas, Texas; 700 to 1,000 in Richmond, Virginia; and 1,000 in Daytona Beach, Florida.[10]

Negro registration reached a minimal level even in the more progressive urban areas of the South after the Populist era.[11] Against this backdrop of negligible registration, more recent levels of Negro political participation can be examined to see what changes have occurred in the political status of Negroes. If we find registration rates to be no longer negligible in some communities of the South, then variables which explain present-day registration will also specify areas of political change since the time of the early 1900's.

In the Matthews and Prothro sample, the percentage of Negroes registered in southern communities varies from 0.0 to 63.4, while the median percentage of Negroes registered is 31.3. (The figures are based upon the percentage of Negroes, sampled in each primary sampling unit, who replied affirmatively to the registration question. Due to high risks of sampling error, five primary sampling units in which the Negro sample is less than 20 have been excluded from these calculations, and, in general from the rest of this study.)

When these more contemporary Negro registration figures are considered against the almost complete removal of Negroes from the registration lists in the early 1900's, it is apparent that important political changes have occurred in some areas of the South.

---

[10] These data are from Lewinson, *Race, Class and Party*, pp. 214–220.

[11] The data gathered by Ralph Bunche for *An American Dilemma* indicate that this was true even in more recent times. Myrdal's conclusion in 1944: "For all practical purposes, Negroes are disfranchised in the South." Myrdal, *An American Dilemma*, p. 475.

Moreover, since the earlier period can be considered roughly the 0-point in Negro registration, the community characteristics of those areas that now have higher registration rates will help specify some aspects of the context in which these changes took place.

The community characteristic most often employed to explain Negro political activity in the South is some measure of the concentration of Negroes.[12] Thus, whites who live in high Negro-density areas, are expected to have the greatest fears of Negro domination. This fear may lead them to limit Negro access to political decision-making. The exclusion of Negroes from the polls is one of the mechanisms by which this can be accomplished.

Two measures of Negro concentration may be useful in explaining Negro registration. One is a contemporary measure, the proportion of Negroes living in the county at the time of the 1960 census.[13] The other is more historical, the county Negro proportion in the 1900 census.[14] If each Negro in the sample is characterized by these two measures, they can be used to explain whether or not he is registered. Table 3-1 indicates the extent to which these variables explain contemporary registration.

The correlations shown in Table 3-1 are the usual product-moment measures of association between variables. The lowest degree of association shown is between Negro proportion in 1900 and Negro registration in 1961; yet the strongest correlation is between Negro proportion in 1900 and in 1960. To a large extent, the same counties that had high concentrations of Negroes in 1900 also had high concentrations in 1960. Moreover, the moderately

---

[12] "And the larger the proportion of Negroes in an area, the more intense the vague fears of Negro domination that seem to beset southern whites. Thus in virtually every study of southern politics, the proportion of Negroes in the population has emerged as a primary explanatory variable." Donald R. Matthews and James W. Prothro, "Social and Economic Factors and Negro Voter Registration in the South," *American Political Science Review,* LVII (1963), 24–44.

[13] This variable was computed for each county that fell into the sample from the state breakdowns reported in U.S. Bureau of the Census, *U.S. Census of Population: 1960. General Social and Economic Characteristics,* Final Report PC (1)-20C (Washington, D.C.: U.S. Government Printing Office, 1961).

[14] This variable is from the Matthews-Prothro study and is on file in the Political Studies Laboratory, Department of Political Science, University of North Carolina, Chapel Hill, N.C.

TABLE 3-1

Intercorrelations and Multiple Correlation between Negro Proportion In 1900 and 1960, and Negro Registration in 1961

	Proportion Negro, 1900	Proportion Negro, 1960	Multiple R
Proportion Negro, 1900		.6846	
Negro Registration, 1961	−.1120	−.3344	.4163

strong correlation between Negro proportion in 1960 and Negro registration in 1961 means that it is in these counties that political discrimination against Negroes persists.

If the multiple correlation is compared to the simple correlation between the Negro proportion in 1960 and Negro registration, the effect of counties that were once high in Negro density, but are no longer as high, can be obtained. The increase in association from .3344 to .4163 indicates that, despite the outmigration of Negroes, a residue of Negro political discrimination remains over and above the amount due to the contemporary Negro concentration.[15] This suggests that, to some extent, patterns of thought and behavior persist over time in a form of social lag, even though the historical facts that gave rise to those patterns no longer exist.

In summing up this string of developments, the following points can be made:

1. Counties that previously witnessed high concentrations of Negroes do not uniformly exhibit violations of minority rights in the contemporary era.

2. Counties that discriminate politically against Negroes in the 1960's are generally the same as those that could have been expected to do so at the turn of the century.

---

[15] This is an individual level dependent variable confirmation of a relationship previously found with aggregate dependent variables in Florida. See H. D. Price, *The Negro and Southern Politics: A Chapter of Florida History* (New York: New York University Press, 1957), p. 41, and Matthews and Prothro, "Social and Economic Factors," pp. 30–31.

3. Because of social lag, less Negro registration exists in the 1960's than would be expected in light of contemporary percentages of Negroes in southern counties.

In general, the relationships between these three variables can be thought of as a developmental sequence from the earlier Negro proportion, to the present proportion, to present registration. As is suggested in point 2 above, registration discrimination in the 1960's exists in that subset of counties that have not varied extensively in Negro density over a period of time. It is the presence of these counties in the sample which accounts for most of the persistence of earlier patterns of race relations.

To a somewhat lesser extent, the summary statement in point 3 includes an additional contribution to this persistence. The phenomena of social lag in race relations, once these relations have been institutionalized, accounts for contemporary patterns that belong to an earlier time.

The major inference brought out by the relationships is that the Negro proportion in 1960 seems to be a contemporary measure of an historical pattern that, except for the additional factor of social lag, represents an inability to fully introduce democratic rules of the game in many communities in the South. Most of the rest of this study will attempt to investigate why this is the case by interpreting the relationship between this apparently historical variable and the index of democratic rules of the game, Negro registration. In so doing, it will attempt to move this relationship up several levels of generalization from an historical generalization to a series of more meaningful propositions for democratic political theory.

SOCIAL FORCES IN SOUTHERN DEMOCRACY

Since the turn of the century, many southern communities have experienced a great deal of social change while others have maintained a fairly stagnant undemocratic pattern. To increase our understanding of why a measure of Negro concentration is able to discriminate between these communities, other indicators of the community setting must be examined. In this study, a series of six measures of county socio-economic characteristics were extracted from the 1960 census and other sources and were conceptualized as attributes of the Negroes sampled in those counties.[16] The intercorrelations between these indicators are shown in Table 3-2.

Of these six indicators, the highest correlations are between percent of labor force in agriculture and the variables: median number of school years, median income, and percent urban. This suggests that these four variables represent alternative measures of the decline of the South's status as a primarily rural, agricultural society. As we go from agricultural to urban communities, we find increases in income and educational attainment.

Only two of the six variables do not follow this pattern. Percent manufacturing is more highly related to median income and percent Roman Catholic than it is to percent of labor in agriculture. Percent Roman Catholic is less highly related to percent in agriculture than it is to almost everything else. In both cases, these relationships are among the weakest of the set.

If these six variables do indeed measure a similar broad dimension of the social setting, then their effect on Negro registration should be a common one. Political scientists normally expect social change to have political consequences. In this case, as industrialization changes economic relations from those based upon ascribed to achieved statuses, a similar effect may be seen among political relationships. Bureaucratization may make more difficult

---

[16] These variables are: percent of county population Roman Catholic (obtained from the Political Studies Laboratory files), percent manufacturing of county's labor force, percent of county population urban, median income in county, median number of school years in county, and percent agriculutre in county's labor force. The latter variables are those most easily computed from U.S. Bureau of the Census, *U.S. Census 1960*. The addition of these variables to the two measures of percent Negro gives us a total of eight independent variables. We should expect some differences between the relationships of these variables to Negro registration in Matthews and Prothro's 1950 census data and our variables from the 1960 census. However, the rank order correlation between the two sets of relationships will indicate how well our sample of counties compares with the South-wide data. This correlation is .833. Two of the variables in the Matthews and Prothro data are computed for non-whites only, since county data for both races combined were not included in that study. If these variables are dropped from the comparison, the rank order correlation reduces to .60. See Matthews and Prothro, "Social and Economic Factors."

TABLE 3-2
Simple Correlations among Six County
Socio-economic Indicators

	(2) Median Number of School Years in County	(3) Median Income in County	(4) Percent Urban of County Population	(5) Percent Manu-facturing of County Labor Force	(6) Percent Roman Catholic of County Population
(1) Percent Agricultural of County's Labor Force	−.8514	−.7963	−.7460	−.2305	.0497
(2) Median Number of School Years in County		.6616	.7363	−.1019	.0054
(3) Median Income in County			.7183	.4408	.2170
(4) Percent Urban of County Population				−.1747	.3579
(5) Percent Manufacturing of County Labor Force					.3454
(6) Percent Roman Catholic of County Population					

the allocation of political statuses based upon non-achievement criteria such as race. Therefore, the social differences measured by the six aggregate variables can be predicted to be correlated to lessened degrees of arbitrary racial discrimination in registration. Moreover, if these variables measure the same dimension, their effect on registration should be the same. Table 3-3 shows the tests of these hypotheses.

TABLE 3-3
Correlations between County Social and Economic
Characteristics, and Individual Negro Registration

County Characteristics	Simple Correlation	Partial Correlation Controlling for Percent Agriculture
(1) *Percent Agricultural of County's Labor Force*	−.4097	
(2) *Median Number of School Years in County*	.3391	−.0173
(3) *Median Income in County*	.3374	.0203
(4) *Percent Urban of County Population*	.2858	−.0326
(5) *Percent Manufacturing of County's Labor Force*	.1732	.0888
(6) *Percent Roman Catholic of County Population*	.0128	.0364

Examining the simple correlations in Table 3-3 shows that, except for percent Roman Catholic, these variables do have the hypothesized effect. The absence of an effect from percent Catholic is interesting because previous studies of Louisiana (and South-wide studies that include the Catholic regions of that state) show Catholicism to bring important gains in Negro political participation.[17] The present sample did not tap any southern Louisiana counties. The absence of a relationship due to percent Catholic therefore indicates that, except for Louisiana, the position of Negro politics in Catholic areas does not differ from that in other southern counties.[18] What is distinctive about Catholic areas in Louisiana can only be guessed. Two possibilities that immediately come to mind are: Catholics have to be in the majority in a community

---

[17] See John H. Fenton and Kenneth N. Vines, "Negro Registration in Louisiana," *American Political Science Review,* LI (1957), 704–713, and Matthews and Prothro, "Social and Economic Factors."

[18] The Matthews-Prothro South-wide aggregate data also contain relationships that suggest this. See Matthews and Prothro, "Social and Economic Factors."

before the more traditional southern norms toward Negroes can be violated. Alternatively, Catholicism is not the important factor at all; but the previously found relationships are really due to ethnic factors that are inseparable concomitants of Catholicism in Louisiana. If future research shows this latter hypothesis to be the operative one, then notions of political and racial values based upon the distinctive Catholic religious dogma can be rejected.

If the correlations in Table 3-3 are compared to the correlations in Table 3-2, we find that the absolute magnitude of the relationships between these variables and Negro registration has the same rank order as their relationship to percent of labor in agriculture. Therefore, while the six variables measure social differences which bring increased tolerance for Negro participation, the similarity in the rank order of relationship suggests that these variables might be reduced to a more parsimonious statement of social change. The strongest variable in the system, percent labor in agriculture, might be used to represent the general effect of industrialization on registration. This can be done only if controlling all relationships by this variable eliminates the other effects. The partial correlations in Table 3-3 show that this is the case. Nearly all the other relationships are dropped back to approximately zero. The effect of percent Catholic increases slightly, however, its effect remains negligible. In general, the partial correlations lead to the inference that the major effect of the social and economic variables on Negro registration is due to change among southern communities. This change seems to be from agricultural societies to more mixed societies resembling, to a large degree, the northern pattern.

If percent of labor in agriculture can be employed as a more parsimonious measure of the common effect of the social and economic differences measured by these variables, then the next step is to examine its relationship with the indicator for the more historical pattern of southern life, the Negro proportion. The simple correlation between them is .6846. Moreover, the multiple correlation between these variables and Negro registration is .4163. Comparing this figure with the correlation between Negro proportion and Negro registration ($-.3344$) indicates that percent of labor in agriculture has some incremental effect on registration over and above that of Negro concentration. This effect is minor, however. The increase in the correlation after adding percent of labor in agriculture is less than .10.[19] At the statistical level of analysis, then, when we relate Negro proportion to registration, we subsume within this relationship the most important influence of percent of labor in agriculture on Negro registration.

These interrelationships are also substantively important. The reason that the historical fact of high Negro concentration in a county continues to play a large role in whether or not Negroes are registered to vote in the county in the 1960's is that the county is likely to have experienced limited economic development. Counties with low densities of Negroes, therefore, may have had the greatest degree of change in their economic and social structure; in these counties Negroes are more likely to register to vote.

Apparently, then, the counties of the South which have generally been the most "Southern" in their characteristics—the counties with a high proportion of Negroes—contain built-in limitations on growth in the non-agricultural sector. What these limitations might be is a matter of speculation for the present study. Several alternative hypotheses can be suggested, however. Perhaps the distribution of natural resources needed for industry is uncorrelated or negatively correlated with agricultural resources. Perhaps the traditional agricultural pattern of southern life restricts the development of a skilled labor pool necessary for modern industry. Perhaps the idyllic image of the South maintained in these counties hampers the creation of local tax and other incentives for industry that are found in other, more competitive southern communities. Perhaps management has determined that the replacement of customary relationships based upon race, by industrial status relationships based on skill or seniority, would be too costly. Perhaps entrenched traditional patterns of race relations present industry with an unacceptably high potential for social instability. Whatever the reasons for this relationship, our assumption is that some counties that were historically agricultural have remained so. If so, we can easily account for the string of relationships ending in Negro registration: other southern counties have developed toward the somewhat more egalitarian pattern characteristic of a modern economy. These speculations suggest that the absolute social distance

---

[19] Again this is a confirmation of an aggregate finding. Matthews and Prothro's aggregate measure of registration is explained by a variety of social factors, but the most important of these is Negro proportion. See *ibid.*

between the high and low density Negro counties has increased rather than diminished over time.

The introduction of socio-economic variables results in a somewhat more fully elaborated understanding of the meaning of the relationship between Negro concentration and Negro registration. An important, perhaps unanticipated, function of the Negro proportion is a more agricultural economy in the contemporary age. Lack of economic development in a county is itself associated with the non-registration of Negroes. Therefore, the reason that Negro concentration continues to correlate with Negro registration is that the former variable may measure relative degrees of modification of general social patterns since the post-Reconstruction era. One element of these patterns is Negro access to the more routine forms of mass level political participation. Thus the counties with a high Negro proportion may more often maintain post-Reconstruction social structures that include the denial of voting rights to Negroes. On the other hand, low density Negro counties seem to have been more likely to accept social structures somewhat characteristic of industrialized America, including a more equalitarian polling booth.

The search for further reasons for these differences in the political status of Negroes is, strictly speaking, a test of the implementation of democracy. After finding the patterns of behavior associated with Negro access to voting in the South, we can begin to make inferences about how democracy becomes institutionalized. The South is an efficient test site for such inferences because of two factors explored in this chapter.

First, large variations have developed among the region's communities in an important dimension of democracy, minority voting rights. These variations permit an analysis in which democracy can be treated as a variable. Although important insights for democratic theory have been gained by treating democracy as a constant, further gains require better measurement procedures. An adequate explanation of democracy, therefore, necessitates that democracy, like any other dependent variable, be measured with sufficient variation so that the degrees of association between it and other variables can be estimated.

Second, this variation in minority voting rights can be specified with a variable that is an indicator of broad patterns of the immediate social setting, Negro proportion. The elaboration here of the logical status of the latter variable indicates that it represents, not only the contemporary density of Negroes in southern counties, but also varying degrees of industrialization. Proportion of population that is Negro can therefore be used as a measure of broad social differences in the context within which the behavior in question takes place.

The political actions that bring about Negro mass participation in the 1960's can be presumed to be derived from earlier social conditions. Although these earlier structures are undoubtedly very complex, the bulk of this chapter indicates that in the American South they can be summarized and simplified by subsuming them under a measure of Negro density such as Negro proportion. This variable will therefore be used as an indicator for a whole array of social background variables that form the historical and contemporary social environments from which existing political patterns have been derived.

When, in the following chapters, we turn to a test of theories of more proximate causes of democracy, Negro proportion will be introduced as the most important independent variable in the system. Thus the peculiar historical developments of the South will be introduced into each test, thereby recognizing the important factors of this specific case for the theory with which we are concerned.

CHAPTER FOUR

Political Stratification
and the Normative Setting

In the previous chapter, aspects of the social structure correlated highly with whether or not Negroes were registered to vote. If the normative context within which Negroes live affects their ability to participate freely in politics, then the attitudes and values of whites in the community in which Negro respondents live should also be related to Negro registration. This possibility raises the intriguing question of whether the social environment and the normative context have independent effects on the dependent variable or whether their effects are interrelated as part of the same stream of effects. If these are independent effects, then the two bodies of partial theory discussed in the second chapter—the socio-economic prerequisites of democracy and the effect of agreement on democratic values— stand as isolated bodies of research. However, if the socio-economic and normative effects are interrelated, then perhaps these research fields can be integrated into a more general model of relationships.

In this analysis the argument has been that the social and economic aspects of the local community are important contextual variables for political behavior. Therefore, if these characteristics relate to behavior that has implications for democratic practices, then their effects might be transmitted through intervening attitudes and values concerning democratic practices. The hypothesis suggested by the contextual approach to democratic theory is that these two different categories of relationships would be interrelated as part of the same stream of contextual effects. More specifically, this notion suggests that the reason that aggregate socio-economic variables are so highly correlated with democratic practices is that such measures are often indicators of cultural homogeneity or the lack thereof. As a result, they may measure the extent to which pressures for conformity are in conflict. It seems reasonable to assume that the more such pressures are in conflict, the lower the costs of deviant behavior. Therefore, the aggregate level relationships often reported may be due to conflict or heterogeneity in values rather than to purely economic sources.

In this and the following chapters we will explore these possibilities. In this chapter we will look at the impact of one type of value in the community context—attitudes toward democracy. Moreover, the particular context under examination will be the white community. Given the fact that politics in the South is dominated by whites, we would expect white attitudes to be a very important factor in political practices as far as the Negro is concerned. Therefore, the interrelationship between socio-economic variables, white attitudes on democracy, and Negro registration will be examined.

DEMOCRATIC ATTITUDES

Measuring democratic values is a difficult task. As indicated in Chapter One, many citizens may have rather nebulous notions of what democracy means. What the respondent subjectively thinks democracy is may be an important datum for many types of research; but when the distribution of objectively defined democratic values is under study, the researcher has to make careful decisions as to which responses are democratic and which are undemocratic.

The best operational definition of democratic values in the literature is that of Prothro and Grigg.[1] The authors set out general principles of democracy and then derive specific values from them. Their item that corresponds to the specific value of Negro political equality is "A Negro should not be allowed to run for Mayor of this city." The item available in the present study which comes closest to measuring the same value is "Colored people ought to be allowed to vote." In this question, the postulated level of Negro participation is much lower. However, the questions are similar in addressing themselves to unrestricted access for the political minor-

---

[1] James W. Prothro and Charles M. Grigg, "Fundamental Principles of Democracy, Bases of Agreement and Disagreement," *Journal of Politics,* XXII (1960), 276–294.

ity to the specific level of participation involved. White agreement to the latter question, therefore, does elicit a measure of adherence to political equality for Negroes.

Given the face validity of the item, a further check on its use in this study is to examine its construct validity. For this purpose, the distribution of responses to the items and their correlates will be examined. White respondents were asked whether they "agree quite a bit, agree a little, disagree a little, or disagree quite a bit" with the item. Only 1.9 percent of the sample either gave no response to the item or replied "don't know," indicating that an extremely large proportion felt that this question had some meaning for them. Seventy-four percent of the rest of the sample agreed quite a bit, 14.7 percent agreed a little, 4.0 disagreed a little, and 7.3 percent disagreed quite a bit. Therefore, those who answered the question nearly achieved a consensus in favor of allowing Negroes to vote. The two disagree responses together account for approximately 11 percent of the entire white sample. Apparently this item so taps the commitment to political equality in the overriding American creed that even southerners find it difficult to disagree with it.

Even given this high degree of commitment to political equality, other studies suggest that differences in the rate of disagreement should show up among levels of political activity.[2] The distribution of the "disagree quite a bit" responses over a political activity index gives the curve illustrated in Figure 4-1.

Figure 4-1 shows that this hypothesis is proved among southern whites. The percentage disagreeing declines from over 13 percent at score I to under 4 percent at score VII. Moreover, this decline is almost monotonic, marred only by slight rises at scores V and VI. The overall trend, then, is that increasingly higher levels of political activity bring lower rates of disagreement on allowing Negroes to vote. This trend is in agreement with other studies of the effect of political stratification on democratic values in the United States.

In addition to the impact of political stratification, the cor-

---

[2] See Herbert McClosky, "Consensus and Ideology in American Politics," *American Political Science Review,* LVIII, 361–382, and Samuel A. Stouffer, *Communism, Conformity, and Civil Liberties* (Garden City: Doubleday, 1955).

relations between the item and other variables that are theoretically predicted to relate to democratic values have been examined. Agreement to this minority rights question is accompanied by lower feelings of anomia, as we would expect. Thus, feelings of estrangement from a society with a democratic public ideology leads to undemocratic predispositions.[3] In addition, agreement to the ques-

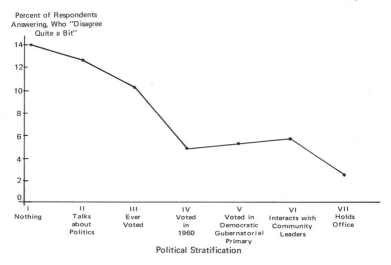

Figure 4-1. Attitude Toward Negro Voting by Levels of Political Stratification

tion is positively correlated with attitude toward change and with level of political information. These are factors which democratic theorists imply to be preconditions for democracy.[4] The item has a negative correlation with attitude toward segregation. Those who favor undemocratic social systems disfavor democratic political systems.

Given some level of validity of this item, the next question is, does it make any difference? That is, do the attitudes it taps

---

[3] For a discussion of the consequences of anomia and related factors see Robert E. Lane, *Political Life* (Glencoe: The Free Press, 1959), pp. 166–169.

[4] See Herbert McClosky, "Conservatism and Personality," *American Political Science Review*, LII (1958), 27–45.

have any impact? Despite the decades of research on political attitudes, we have very little information on the relationship between these attitudes and the natures of political systems or even between them and other behaviors of the individuals measured. In the field of measuring democratic attitudes, the assumption that these attitudes have an impact on the system needs empirical support. This is especially the case in that, to the extent that we have any inferences on the impact of these attitudes, the predominate thinking is in the negative, as the discussion of the consensus literature in the previous chapter indicates.

If we aggregate white attitudes on the Negro participation item for each primary sampling unit, we can treat this variable as part of the community context for Negroes living in that P.S.U. The correlation between this variable and Negro registration can then be examined to see if this aspect of the community context has the predicted effect. In the South this correlation is .274. Although this is not a spectacularly large correlation, it is a respectable one. In other words, where whites' opinion in the aggregate is most receptive to free political participation on the part of Negroes, there is some tendency for Negroes to be more likely to become registered. The normative context as far as the white community is concerned *does* have some impact on the local political practice. However, this tendency is not an extremely strong one, and it is possible that this pattern is only a minor one among all the factors explaining democracy.

Nevertheless, the finding is in sharp contrast with the conventional wisdom gained from a simple-minded reading of the consensus literature. The usual presumption is that the conclusion that democratic consensus at the popular level has no impact also means that popular attitudes have no impact. This finding leads us to rethink the latter statement. In short, it shows the utility of the distinction between consensus and degree of agreement which was made in the second chapter.

The finding, however, is still at a tentative stage, and we cannot rush to the conclusion that these attitudes have the hypothesized impact. Further elaboration of the relationship may lend support to it. It is necessary to pay close attention to theoretical grounds for choosing variables that specify the conditions under which the relationship occurs.

One reason for the rather low relationship is that it is possible that not all whites have the same role in structuring the norms of the community. In simply computing the aggregate opinion, we assign all whites an equal force in developing the rules of the game. If we could isolate those who might have a greater impact, we could weight white opinions differentially, thereby increasing the correlation. In the following discussion we will consider arguments on how to stratify the white population in political terms in order to test this hypothesis.

POLITICAL STRATIFICATION

One of the major reasons way scholars and ordinary citizens are interested in the relationship between higher and lower political strata is that they usually feel that such relationships influence the outcomes of the political system. The governmental practices that affect our lives may vary according to the strength of this relationship. In democratic theory, as we have seen, a high order of relationship between these strata is expected. Because of this strong relationship, governmental outcomes are then hypothesized to have some degree of popular support.

In contrast to these expectations, much empirical research leads to doubts that all these linkages exist even under more or less democratic conditions. The study of public opinion in the United States shows fairly low levels of popular knowledge on specific policy issues.[5] Moreover, the study of the rules of the game, which structure the conditions within which issue discussions take place, illuminates the low popular adherence to democratic practices.[6] If the less politically active ("inactivists") have low agreement to democracy, how can their relationship with the more politically active stratum affect the degree of democracy which characterizes political systems? One answer to this question is that the inactivists are hardly involved at all in setting the rules of the

---

[5] See Angus Campbell, Phillip Converse, Warren E. Miller, and Donald E. Stokes, *The American Voter* (New York: Wiley & Sons, 1960), pp. 541–548.

[6] Samuel A. Stouffer, *Communism, Conformity*.

game. This answer has an implicit emphasis on the role of the upper political stratum as the major factor producing or maintaining the rules of the game.[7]

The derivation of the hypothesis in Chapter One considered the thinking that holds that democratic agreement among the more politically active stratum is the crucial factor for such maintenance. That thinking developed out of a stream of literature in which the dependent variable, democratic rules of the game, was constant.[8] Thus a political system that followed more or less democratic practices—usually the United States—was tested for distributions of democratic values within its population. If something less than a consensus on democratic values existed in the population at large, then such a consensus could not be said to be necessary in order to maintain democracy. Also, if a consensus on these values was more fully approximated among political activists than among the population at large, then there were strong suggestions that consensus at this level may have been the crucial factor.

Despite the importance for democratic theory of the relationship between various strata and the rules of the game, very little progress has been made toward constructing comparative tests of the relationship. A major reason for the lack of progress here is the phenomenal difficulty of conceptualizing and measuring political stratification. For example, students of community decision-making engage in heated discussions over alternative methods to

---

[7] A somewhat more restrained position is that articulated by V. O. Key, Jr.: "That at times mass opinion may handicap desirable action cannot be denied. Yet as one puzzles over the nature of interactions between government and mass opinion and ponders such empirical data as can be assembled on the matter, he can arrive only at the conclusion that a wide range of discretion exists for whatever wisdom leadership echelons can muster in the public service. The generality of public preferences, the low intensity of the opinions of many people, the low level of political animosities of substantial sectors of the public, the tortuousness of the process of translation of disapproval of specific policies into electoral reprisals, and many other factors point to the existence of a wide latitude for the exercise of creative leadership." V. O. Key, Jr., *Public Opinion and American Democracy* (New York: Knopf, 1961), p. 555.

[8] Prothro and Grigg, "Fundamental Principles"; Stouffer, *Communism, Conformity*; Robert A. Dahl, *Who Governs?* (New Haven, Conn.: Yale University Press, 1961); Key, *Public Opinion*; and McClosky, "Conservatism and Personality."

measure community power and influence.[9] Although there is a considerable overlap between the positions in this discussion, the main disagreement is between the advocates of measurement by tracing out those who have reputations as being powerful and the advocates of using participation in decision-making as a measure. A similar debate is being waged among students of organizational theory. In that field, notions of authority based upon formal lines of command are being challenged by the results of analyses of the importance of informal interaction and influence in organizational decision-making.[10] These cleavages are crosscut by a third discussion of whether power is an attribute that resides in individuals and roles or whether it is a relationship arising out of the interaction between individuals and roles.[11]

Eventually, these difficulties will undoubtedly be resolved, and a consensus will be reached on ways to discriminate operationally between the more powerful and the less powerful. Until that time, answers to the question of the relationship between strata will be tentative. However, preliminary answers may be suggested by using alternative measures. This procedure may even make it possible to choose between measures on pragmatic grounds such as which approach solves problems most effectively.

One alternative that may help resolve these controversies is to utilize levels of political activity to differentiate individuals into political strata. Thus the present study is based upon a conceptualization of a dimension of political activity along which individuals may be placed.[12] Individuals near the top of the dimension are viewed as leaders and those at the bottom are viewed as the in-

---

[9] For an insightful synthesis of this literature see Nelson W. Polsby, *Community Power and Political Theory* (New Haven, Conn. Yale University Press, 1963). For a combined approach see Robert E. Agger, Daniel Goldrich, Bert E. Swanson, *The Rulers and the Ruled* (New York: Wiley & Sons, 1964).

[10] For one of the first statements of this nature see Phillip Selznick, "Foundations of the Theory of Organization," *American Sociological Review,* XIII (1948), 25–35.

[11] See Richard M. Emerson, "Power-Dependence Relations," *American Sociological Review,* XXVII (1960), 31–41, and Richard Neustadt, *Presidential Power* (New York: Wiley & Sons, 1960).

[12] Key also uses political activity or participation as a measure of political stratification. His justification for doing so has much appeal: "Among large groups we should expect the weight of opinion to vary

activists. Of course, cross-sectional samples, such as that sample analyzed here, include few individuals in the leadership level. Therefore, inferences based upon these data cannot refer to leaders and followers, but only to relative degrees of activity.

Despite this limitation, a focus on political activity places the study of political strata within a framework that is increasingly accepted by scholars. This framework is based upon the concept of a world that is made up of systems of interrelated political activities.[13] These activities together give rise to system-level decisions or authoritative allocations of rewards and deprivations. A stratification dimension can be introduced into this viewpoint by acknowledging qualitative differences among political activities; that is, some activities can be presumed to be more consequential than others in bringing about authoritative allocations of value. Those who engage in these higher level activities can be ranked in a higher stratum than those who do not. Thus, an individual's rank on the political stratification dimension depends upon the qualitative ranking of the political activities he engages in.

The construction of qualitative rankings seems a difficult task, but social scientists' development of Guttman scaling techniques has made this a fairly straightforward procedure.[14] Matthews and Prothro, for example, discovered that political activity tends to be unidimensional.[15] Individuals who hold office are also likely to participate at successively less intensive levels of activity such as campaigning, voting, and talking about politics. Several of the Matthews and Prothro scalar types have been used in this study.[16]

---

roughly with degree of participation as well as with numbers. An assumption to the contrary could rest only on the hypothesis that mass political activity affects the course of events not at all." Key, *Public Opinion*, p. 555.

[13] For the basic statement of this view of the political world see David Easton, "An Approach to the Analysis of Political Systems," *World Politics*, IX (1957), 383–400.

[14] For the procedure used here see Robert N. Ford, "A Rapid Scoring Procedure for Scaling Attitude Questions," *Public Opinion Quarterly*, XV (1960), 507–532.

[15] See Donald R. Matthews and James W. Prothro, *Negroes and the New Southern Politics* (New York: Harcourt, Brace & World, 1966), Chap. 2.

[16] These are: doing nothing about politics, talking about politics, ever voting, and holding office.

However, others have been added here, since the distribution on the original scale of political activity is unimodal. In this study we wish to dichotomize political activity into categories of those who are more active and those who are less active. This classification makes it necessary to have enough additional items to form a bimodal distribution. The levels of political activity have been given in Figure 4-1. The distribution of activities among white southerners is given in Figure 4-2.

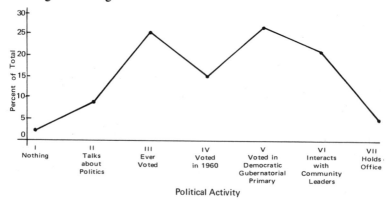

Figure 4-2. Distribution of Political Activity among White Southerners

The types of political activities included in Figures 4-1 and 4-2 as scale scores I, II, III, and VII are items reported by Matthews and Prothro. In addition, the items measuring voting in 1960, voting in the latest Democratic gubernatorial primary, and interacting with community leaders are included. Voting in 1960 is conceived of as a slightly more difficult task for the average citizen than ever voting, since it requires participation in the most recent presidential election. A respondent may have voted in one or more elections in the past in order to qualify for scale score III, but his level of political involvement must have remained high for him to qualify for scale score IV. Moreover, this respondent may be hypothesized to have greater effect on political outcomes than an infrequent voter. Similarly, voting in Democratic gubernatorial primaries is a form of activity which should bring even greater impact on system-level decisions. This presumption is based upon the fact that, functionally speaking, the Democratic primary is the gubernatorial election in most southern states. Therefore, this activity is a "harder" one in the stratification dimension in the South, although this may not be true elsewhere. Interacting with community leaders would seem to be an even more active form of political participation. Face-to-face communication with community leaders is achieved by few citizens, yet those who do reach this level of activity have met a condition which may permit them to bring to bear real influence. Individuals who might have even more influence are those corresponding to scale score VII, the actual participants in day-to-day decision-making, political office-holders.

The crucial test of these statements, however, is whether these forms of activity meet Guttman requirements of cumulative uni-dimensionality. The Matthews and Prothro portion of the dimension scale has already been reported. If only the three items added here are tested for unidimensionality, the coefficient of reproducibility is .944, well above the minimum requirement of .90. If all seven items are included, the coefficient is even higher. Also, the much more stringent coefficient of scalability is .72, again above the .65 minimum. However, the bimodal nature of the distribution indicates that these activities may not meet one of the Guttman requirements, that of randomly distributed errors. There are many individuals who participate at level V who do not participate at level IV. These individuals represent scalar errors resulting from the bimodal nature of the distribution. Therefore, as the downward plunge at scale score IV shows, the errors are somewhat systematically distributed. The important point, however, is that the degree of reproducibility of the dimension demonstrates that these items measure a pattern of cumulatively increasing intensities of political activity. This index will thus be utilized as measuring qualitatively different political activities along a dimenson of political stratification. Since the distribution is bimodal, those at scores V and above are considered among the upper stratum and categorized as activists, and those below V are considered as the less active populace.

Scale score V represents the activity of voting in Democratic gubernatorial primaries. Dividing the sample at this level raises the possibility that the activist category underrepresents Republicans as an artifact of scale construction. A check on this possibility shows that dichotomization at this level does not underrepresent Republicans. Thus, of the total sample of 694 respondents, we now have 343 activists and 351 inactivists.

A necessary disclaimer here is that the index goes only a short distance up the political stratification dimension. There is a possibility that it may not be related to other variables in the same manner as it would be if more participants at even higher levels had been included. This is a problem faced by many studies that attempt to compare different political strata.

EFFECTS OF DEMOCRATIC VALUES AMONG POLITICAL STRATA

A second examination of the contextual effect is whether or not the degree of democratic agreement between white activists and inactivists is related to the practice of political equality in the South. These relationships will then stand for the effects on the rules of the game of activist and popular agreement to political equality. An evaluation of these effects will lead to inferences of whether activist or popular agreement is more important in producing political equality for the Negro minority.

The effects of activist and popular agreement to democratic norms can be evaluated if the aggregated activist and popular agreement variables are treated as independent variables explaining Negro registration. We can now conceptualize agreement to democratic norms among white activists and inactivists in the primary sampling unit as a characteristic of the Negro respondent living in the P.S.U. We can then ask what effect activist agreement and popular agreement in his community has on whether or not he is registered. Figure 4-3 gives the correlations for all possible links between these variables.

Figure 4-3 includes the possibility of a reciprocal influence

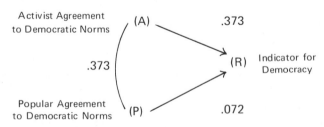

Figure 4-3. Relationships between Democracy and Popular Agreement and Activist Agreement to Democratic Norms

between activist and popular agreement to democratic norms. The nature of these relationships is not under examination here, but the relationship between these variables and dependent variable, Negro registration, is.

The extremely weak relationship between popular agreement and the dependent variable means that that link can be ignored as far as these data are concerned. However, the comparative strength of the other two correlations suggests that there may be a direct effect of popular attitudes which is negative in sign rather than positive when the effect of activist attitudes is controlled. That is, if these relationships were the only possible effects in this system of variables, with A showing a positive correlation, the absence of a correlation between R and P could be due to a negative correlation between P and R if A and P are also positively correlated. The data show a positive correlation between A and P, so the partial or direct effects of the independent variables should be examined.

The links between the independent and dependent variables can be tested to evaluate whether or not they are direct effects.[17] Table 4-1 gives these tests. Prediction equation 1 indicates that the

TABLE 4-1
**Prediction Equations and Degrees of Fit between Activist
Agreement and Popular Agreement to Democratic Norms
and Negro Registration As an Indicator for Democracy**

Prediction Equations	Actual		Predicted	Difference
1. $rAR = rPA\ rPR$	.373	(.373)(.072)	.027	.346
2. $rPR = rAP\ rAR$	.072	(.373)(.373)	.139	−.067

link between activist norms and democracy cannot be rejected. Prediction equation 2, as we would expect, shows that the extremely weak link between popular agreement and democracy can be rejected. This analysis leaves only the assumed reciprocal link between the independent variables and the link between activist

---

[17] We are using the Blalock-Simon technique to evaluate causal models. See Hubert J. Blalock, Jr., *Causal Inferences in Non-experimental Research* (Chapel Hill: University of North Carolina Press, 1964).

agreement and the dependent variable. These relationships are illustrated in Figure 4-4.

The over-prediction obtained for the popular agreement–dependent variable link (a prediction of .139 as opposed to the actual correlation of .072) may indicate a negative partial relationship between the two variables. However, the difference is so small that it could be due to sampling error. Therefore, the possibility of a negative relationship cannot be supported with the evidence at hand.

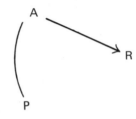

Figure 4-4. Direct Effects between Democracy and Popular and Activist Agreement to Democratic Norms

Figure 4-4 illustrates the inference drawn from these data—that the inactivists do not have a direct effect on the rules of the game, at least insofar as the rules apply to political democracy for Negroes. Instead, among these variables, the higher political stratum has the only direct influence on how democratic the local political system is.[18] If the inactivists had an effect, it would depend upon their influence upon the activists. Under this hypothesis, members of the higher stratum would have two functions. They would stand midway in a path of influence from the inactivists to themselves to democracy; however, since there may be a double arrow between the activists and the inactivists, the higher stratum would also have an additional direct influence on popular level agreement and on the rules of the game. Figure 4-5 breaks the reciprocal relationship into two unicausal paths to illustrate the two functions of the activist level.

The two models in Figure 4-5 show the hypothesis of the possible functions of the politically active in these data. In Model

---

[18] This finding is consistent with the inference suggested by McClosky's data. McClosky, "Consensus and Ideology."

4-5a activist agreement is an intervening variable within a developmental sequence from popular agreement, to activist agreement, to the local rules of the game. On the other hand, Model 4-5b illustrates the impact of the activist level which is independent of the effect of the inactivists. That model suggests that the upper stratum produces democratic rules of the game. Therefore, the democratic character of the local political system could depend upon both processes. It could partially depend upon the extent of activist agreement which is produced by the extent of agreement among the inactivists, and partially dependent upon the extent of democratic agreement among the activists regardless of the level of popular agreement.

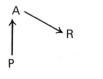

Model 4-5. Effects of the
Inactive Populace on Activists
and Activists on Democracy

Model 4-5. Effects of
Activists on the Inactive
Populace and on Democracy

Figure 4-5. Models of Two Activist Functions in the Relationship between Democratic Norms and Democratic Rules of the Game

However, if level of activist agreement were truly an intervening variable between popular agreement and the dependent variable, there would be some correlation between popular agreement and the rules of the game. The absence of such a correlation leads to the inference that, although popular and activist agreement on our measure of democratic values are correlated, this correlation does not appear to be part of a developmental sequence that gives popular attitudes an influence on the rules of the game. They may influence the activists, but apparently not enough for that influence to carry over to a linear effect on the manner in which the local system deals with Negro registration. The conclusion most warranted by the evidence is that the rules of the game are primarily a function of the attitudes of the activists and that any possible impact of the less active citizens is either lost because of their inactivity or is dampened because of the interaction of their values with those of the activists. Whatever the intervening process may be which accounts for this outcome, the inference remains that the operative rules of the game for Negro registration in the South appear to be free of any direct influence from those whites who are politically inactive.

One possible meaning that we can give to this relationship is that the active citizens, in some sense, "more truly" represent the attitudes of the South. That is, they appear to have more influence because their attitudes more closely correspond to the variations in the general attitudes in the population throughout the South, while the attitudes of the inactivists show less variation. This explanation is an alternative to that implicitly adopted by the arguments thus far—that the greater association is due to the greater political activity of the activists.

Either one or both of these explanations could be true. One way to approximate a test of the possibilities is to examine whether the attitudes of both strata are derived in any sense from socioeconomic variables, or whether the attitudes of either one or both strata are independent of those measures. The argument in the previous chapter was that Negro density stands for variation in "Southernness." We would then expect the activists' attitudes to be more fully articulated with this variable if these attitudes are more representative of the cultural variations relative to treatment of Negroes.

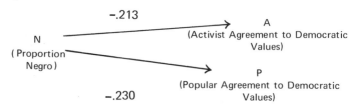

Figure 4-6. The Effect of Negro Proportion on Activist Agreement and Popular Agreement to Democratic Values

Figure 4-6 gives the correlation between Negro concentration and the attitudes of each strata. These relationships are based upon the non-aggregated individual white responses to the democratic attitude question. Therefore, Negro density in the surrounding community is now being viewed as a part of the context for the individual whites. The upper arrow in Figure 4-6 gives the resulting correlation between the Negro proportion and agreement to democratic values among the activists. The lower one indicates the relationship between Negro proportion and agreement to these values among the inactivists. Interestingly enough, these relationships are of about the same magnitude. They are not surprisingly strong, but are in the expected direction—where Negro density is greatest, white attitudes are the least democratic. The inference, then, is that the reason that the rules of the game work against Negro participation in areas of greatest Negro density is because of the behavior of the activists in those areas. The attitudes of both activists and inactivists are shaped by the community context. However, the attitudes of the less active sectors have few consequences for Negroes; the attitudes of the more active citizens have important effects indeed.

A problem related to this is the question of whether or not there are any factors that may compete with this aspect of the community environment in shaping white attitudes. Likely candidates for this role are those variables that measure the individual's socio-economic status. Even within a community, there are usually important variations in individuals' beliefs depending upon differential socialization patterns among social statuses.[19] Therefore, social status may be added to Negro proportion to measure the general relationship between social background and democratic norms. Table 4-2 gives the correlations between Negro proportion, three socio-economic status variables (education, occupation, and income level), and democratic values at popular and activist levels.

Table 4-2 indicates that the three individual social status indicators for white popular and activist levels are relatively uncorrelated with Negro proportion. On the other hand, these variables are somewhat correlated with the strength of agreement to democratic values. The degree of this relationship varies with the particular status factor, with income level being slightly more highly related than the others. The multiple correlation between all three factors and democratic values is .296 and .191 for activist and popular levels respectively. As the proportions in the bottom row of the table indicate, income by itself accounts for most of these combined relationships. Income level, then, can be used as an indicator for the general level of the individual's social status. Since this indicator is practically uncorrelated with Negro proportion, the multiple correlation between the dependent variable and both

---

19 See Prothro and Grigg, "Fundamental Principles."

TABLE 4-2

Relationships between Socio-economic Status Variables, and Negro Proportion and Democratic Values—by Activist and Popular Levels

	Activist Level			Popular Level		
	Educa-tion	Occupa-tion	Income	Educa-tion	Occupa-tion	Income
Negro Proportion	.058	.007	.040	.082	.119	.037
Democratic Values	.192	.247	.253	.154	.132	.155
Proportion of Multiple R[a]	.649	.834	.855	.806	.691	.812

[a] The simple correlations between each status indicator and democratic values divided by the multiple correlation between all three status indicators and democratic values.

of these social background factors should be greater than the simple correlation between Negro proportion and the dependent variable. Figure 4-7 shows these new correlations.

Figure 4-7. Combined Effect of Negro Proportion and Income on Activist Agreement and Popular Agreement to Democratic Values

A comparison of the multiple correlations shown in Figure 4-7 with the simple correlations between Negro proportion and democratic values indicates that income has a much greater effect on activist values than on popular values. In the case of the activists, adding income increases the correlation from .213 to .338. At the popular level, the increase is only from .230 to .293. Democratic norms at the activist level—to a much greater extent than at the popular level—are independently influenced by differences in social status. Thus, one of the reasons activists adhere to democratic norms is their higher social status. This relationship occurs irrespective of the differences due to community environments of the activists. Individual characteristics, therefore, have an impact on white attitudes, especially those of the activists, over and above that of the community context.

CONCLUSIONS

In this chapter we have explored some further implications of what we have termed the contextual hypothesis. One resulting inference is: The fact that whites are less socialized to democratic values in communities of high Negro density accounts for the fact that the registration of individual Negroes has been found to vary with a community characteristic such as Negro density. White attitudes toward democracy, then, have an impact on whether or not Negroes are able to participate in politics by registering. Moreover, as we would expect from previous research, the relationship between white attitudes and the rules of the game with respect to Negroes is higher for white activists than for inactivists. Whatever the processes of interaction between the attitudes of the more active and the less active whites, the data from one point in time show little relationship between the attitudes of the less active sectors and the rules of the game. It would appear, therefore, that we cannot only interpret the Negro proportion–Negro registration relationship with white attitudes, but that we can, in addition, specify white activist attitudes as the most important factor in the sequence.

Yet if white attitudes serve as the context for Negro behavior —and, ironically, Negro concentration serves as the context for white attitudes—we cannot conclude that contextual effects are the only operative ones. The social status of white citizens also has important consequences for democratic attitudes and, thus, for the rules of the game. However, the impact of social status has been an important element in the *conventional* wisdom concerning democratic values and the rules of the game. Therefore, new conclusions which result are a result of the effect of the wider community context that exists almost independently and in addition to the social status of the individual.

Our guesses about the historical meaning of Negro concentration, when added to these findings, suggest that active and inactive whites are equally socialized to southern traditions. The danger in this socialization, as far as Negroes are concerned, lies primarily in the higher probability that the attitudes of the activists will be acted upon in some way. The contemporary consequences of the southern tradition tend to be due to the role of the higher strata as carriers of this particular socio-political creed—a creed that thereby serves as part of the normative context for many southern Negroes.

Nevertheless, the evidence should not be read as indicating that mass values do not have an effect on the rules of the game as practiced in the South. Although the relationship exists only when we examine the values of the higher political strata, the fact remains that these are not elites. They are citizens who fall into a survey sample drawn to be representative of the voting population; they are politically active only in a relative sense. Therefore, the general conclusion that must be drawn is in contradiction with much previous theorizing. At least in the South, mass attitudes are related to the rules of the game, even if the effect is nonexistent for the most inactive citizens. This may mean that when the existing rules of the game are challenged by the wider national ideology, the rules will be more consistent with that ideology when active citizens more fully internalize the norms as their own.

CHAPTER FIVE

The Individual
and the Normative Setting

Although the normative context may influence whether or not black southerners become registered, we cannot be sure that we have adequately measured this influence until additional patterns and trends have been taken into consideration. In this chapter we will examine the impact of the personal characteristics of Negroes such as social status and political involvement—characteristics that may relate to registration quite separately from our contextual hypothesis. Also, some very rough indicators of the political structure, such as political violence, will be introduced. Finally, all of the major variables on which the study focuses will be related simultaneously to the dependent variable.

The argument in the previous chapter—that white attitudes in the community, especially those attitudes of the more politically active citizens, are related to whether or not Negroes become registered—may bear some further examination. For example, the main thrust of the argument has been that the dependent variable serves as a rough indicator for political equality and, therefore, for democracy. In making this rough equation between Negro registration and democracy, we may be understating the level of democracy in the South. The past decade of voting behavior research indicates that there are purely individualistic reasons why people do not vote and (by inference) do not become registered.[1] In general, citizens of lower social status are less likely to bother about voting and other forms of traditional political activity. One of the intervening

---

[1] See Campbell, *et al., The American Voter* (New York: Wiley & Sons, 1960) or just about any other voting study.

factors here is the low level of psychological involvement in politics which lower status citizens have; high involvement seems to be part of a more middle class outlook on citizenship.

In the case of the South we would expect Negro social status and psychological involvement to affect Negro registration. Therefore, these variables would have to be introduced explicitly in order to obtain a proper reading of the level of political equality and, as a consequence, the independent effect of democratic attitudes among whites.

A test of one alternative process that may account for Negro registration is just one type of elaboration needed on the relationship between white community sentiment and the dependent variable. In addition, even assuming that the dependent variable is an adequate measure of democracy, it is not immediately clear in just what way white attitudes in the community impinge upon Negro behavior. In other words, we want to identify the intervening variables that account for this relationship. Such elaborations will be attempted in this chapter. While few definitive answers can be given, some preliminary answers can be suggested concerning the way in which activist sentiment relates to Negro registration.

NEGRO POLITICAL INVOLVEMENT AND POLITICAL PARTICIPATION

Since the dependent variable which serves as an indicator for democracy is a form of political participation, we may have to take additional variables into consideration in order to measure accurately the effect of the (white) community context on the rules of the game. Negro registration rates may overstate the extent to which southern communities are undemocratic. There may be many reasons why people fail to participate in politics by not registering to vote; the existence of oppressive rules of the game is just one of these. To form a more accurate indicator for the dependent variable, these other factors need to be estimated and controlled.

The other confounding factors that need to be controlled are those purely individual motivations to participate in politics.[2] In

---

[2] For a general discussion of the findings relating social status to

other words, an individual may not participate, not because he is restricted somehow by the local context, but because he is not interested or concerned with politics, or because he has not been socialized to the norm of democratic participation. Factors such as these have been measured in the United States in previous studies. They tend to have great variability among individuals and seem to be due to differential socializing experiences. Since it can be hypothesized that southern Negroes will tend to have lower levels of these motivational factors, they may fail to become registered for purely individual reasons—reasons that would interfere with the measure of the community effect. An index of political involvement has been constructed for the Negro sample to serve as an overall indicator for these motivational factors. The components of the measure are conceptually similar to those of previous measures of involvement.[3] These are: interest in politics, intensity of party identification, and the sense of the responsiveness of the political world.

As we would expect from previous research, this composite variable has a rather high correlation (.544) with the dependent variable. Therefore, this variable explains Negro registration to a much greater extent than does the community context variable. If

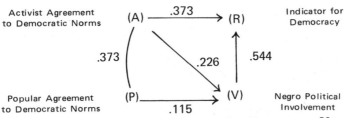

Figure 5-1. Relationships among Indicator for Democracy, Negro Political Involvement, Activist Agreement, and Popular Agreement to Democratic Norms

we take the effects of political involvement into consideration in the model of relationships presented in the previous chapter, we have the relationships illustrated in Figure 5-1.

In Figure 5-1 there is no link between P and R. The intro-

---

individual motivations to participation, see Robert E. Lane, *Political Life* (Glencoe, Ill.: The Free Press, 1959), pp. 196–197.

[3] See Campbell, *et al.*, *The American Voter*, pp. 59–60.

duction of the new variable does not upset the earlier finding that rPR can be accounted for by the relationships between A and P and A and R. Four other links can be hypothesized to be without direct effects. The correlation between A and R may be accounted for by the sequence of rAV and rVR. Alternatively, rVR may be accounted for by rAV and rAR. The correlation between A and V may possibly be accounted for by rAP and rPV. On the other hand, rAV and rAP may remove rPV. Table 5-1 gives the prediction equations and degrees of fit for these hypotheses.

TABLE 5-1
Prediction Equations and Degrees of Fit for the Four-Variable Case
Produced by Adding Negro Political Involvement to the Model

Prediction Equations	Actual		Predicted	Difference
1. rAR = rAV rVR	.373	(.226)(.544)	.123	.250
2. rVR = rAV rAR	.544	(.226)(.373)	.084	.460
3. rAV = rAP rPV	.226	(.373)(.115)	.043	.183
4. rPV = rAV rAP	.115	(.226)(.373)	.084	.031

The large differences between the actual and predicted correlations for prediction equations 1, 2, and 3 means that the links corresponding to rAR, rVR, and rAV cannot be rejected. Instead, these links can be inferred to have direct effects. The small difference for Prediction equation 4, on the other hand, means that rPV can be rejected. Therefore, we can infer that the inactivists have no direct effect on Negro political involvement. The factor directly influencing Negro involvement among these relationships is activist agreement to democratic norms. Any influence the inactivists may have on the Negro's motivations to participate is indirect, working through the inactivists' impact on activist agreement.

THE EFFECT OF DEMOCRATIC VALUES ON NEGRO INVOLVEMENT

The inferences made above again illustrate the importance of the activist stratum in the operation of the political system. The most important political factor producing Negro registration is found at the activist level. Also, democratic agreement at that level has some association with Negro motivations toward types of participa- tion such as registration. The popular stratum, however, may not be without some impact on Negro involvement. Since there may be a reciprocal relationship between activist and popular norms, the sequence from inactivists, to activists, to Negro involvement could provide the inactivists with a secondary influence on the participation motivations of Negroes. These relationships make up a new model that is derived from the analysis in Table 5-1. The new model is shown in Figure 5-2.

Figure 5-2. Direct Effects between Democracy and Negro Political Involvement, and Activist Agreement, and Popular Agreement to Democratic Norms

Figure 5-2 suggests that there are two paths of influence from activist agreement to democratic norms to the indicator for democracy. One is a direct linkage running from A to R. The other is an indirect path from A to V to R. The latter relationship is in direct support of much socio-psychological thinking. Normally, a form of behavior, such as a Negro becoming registered, is viewed as a culmination of psychological forces pushing the individual toward that behavior. Some of the more impressive research on American voting behavior supports this view.[4] Also, the factors explaining the cumulative scale of Negro participation developed by Matthews and Prothro are mediated through the Negro's political attitudes and perceptions.[5] We should, therefore, expect the impact of the activists' attitudes in the community on Negro registration to be interpreted by the Negro's psychological predisposition to participate. While this expectation may not be entirely

---

[4] *Ibid.*

[5] See Donald R. Matthews and James W. Prothro, *Negroes and the New Southern Politics* (New York: Harcourt, Brace & World, 1966), Chap. 11.

fulfilled, as is shown by the direct link between A and R, the A to V relationship indicates that the psychological orientation of Negroes does account for a portion of the effect of the community context.

There are two conclusions suggested by Figure 5-2, each of which involves further elaboration of the relationships given there. First, it is not accurate to control only for the effects of involvement in order to measure the effects of the white community. To an extent, part of the reason that the white community has the effect that it has is that Negroes apparently go through experiences in their communities which lead to low motivations toward participation. In a sense, the psychological state of Negroes has adapted to the prevailing restrictiveness among local whites. Therefore, involvement is not fully determined by purely individual characteristics. We can think of two types of forces which are transmitted by Negro involvement, the restrictiveness of the white community and the more purely individual characteristics of Negroes. The idea of controlling the effect of involvement in order to measure the effect of the community is erroneous because part of the community effect seems to be transmitted through involvement. The strategy that must be adopted is one of finding a more purely individual measure of Negro social experience which is also transmitted through involvement. We can then sort out to what extent involvement is due to this variable, on the one hand, and due to the nature of the white community on the other hand.

Second, we can pursue the notion that there is a direct effect from white activist attitudes which is not transmitted through Negro involvement. The residual relationship, after involvement is taken into account, is small and, therefore, may be due to extraneous factors such as measurement error. Yet we can think of perfectly good theoretical reasons for expecting such a direct effect. Although it is not possible to find conclusive evidence on the problem, a strategy that may provide some answers is the complement of that described above: to try to find indicators for the variables that intervene between the community context variable and Negro registration, but that are *not* related to Negro involvement. This elaboration will be carried out in the next section; the one following that one will elaborate upon the impact of involvement.

POLITICAL STRUCTURE AND
POLITICAL PARTICIPATION

The inference that white attitudes concerning democracy have an impact suggests the importance of political structures in explaining the dependent variable. For most Americans political behavior, like voting, is to a large degree within the control of the individual's motivations. Whether or not the individual engages in this behavior is up to him. For the southern Negro, however, this is not the case. In many communities his political behavior is restricted by white sentiments, but the restrictive nature of the locality does not affect all types of Negro participation equally. Several factors in the Matthews and Prothro scale seem to be free of these restrictions. Negroes may talk about politics with other Negroes without encountering the wrath of the white community. Other less visible forms of participation, such as supporting candidates through campaign contributions, may similarly be freely engaged in. In these areas of participation, apathy or lack of involvement would be the primary limiting factors. Social and political structures may affect these forms of participation only by affecting psychological predispositions. The inclusion of these types of behavior in the scale of Negro participation increases the degree to which social-psychological variables intervene between the more independent variables and the scale.

To the extent that behavior is free of restrictions imposed from outside the individual, psychological factors tend to be the most important forces involved. But to the extent that external restrictions are imposed, they tend to operate more directly on the behavior, independent of the individual's attitudes and perceptions. Chapter Three pointed out the ease with which registration can be manipulated by governmental agencies. Registration of Negroes is thus highly vulnerable to a restrictive administration. Figure 5-2 suggests that the extent of restrictive sentiment among white leaders may influence a Negro's chances to become registered, despite his level of involvement. This would mean that even when Negroes are highly involved they cannot become registered if whites in their community have low levels of agreement to democratic values.

Further tests of these inferences can be carried out by considering additional categories of data. The relationships between the variables in the model and measures of the formal and informal political structure which affect Negro registration can be investigated. Many of these aspects of the southern political structure have been found to relate to Negro registration.[6] In communities in which acts of racial violence occurred and literacy tests existed, Negro registration rates tended to be lower than in similar communities without these characteristics. On the other hand, in communities in which there is a bifactional Democratic party structure and in which a gubernatorial candidate tends to be favorable to Negroes, Negro registration rates are higher. The inference that these political practices limit or increase Negro registration rates can be drawn into the discussion of the effect of activist norms on Negro political equality.

If activist norms could affect the registration of Negroes to a greater extent than it does Negro political involvement, then those aspects of the political structure which restrict Negro participation should also be more highly related to registration than to involvement. In other words, as white activist norms vary in their restrictiveness toward Negro participation, so should *indicators* for political and administrative practices that limit Negro participation. If the effect of activist norms is greater on Negro registration than on Negro political involvement, then these political practices should have a similar effect.

The first test of these hypotheses is to investigate whether or not the aspects of the political structure considered have the same effect on our measure of Negro registration as they did on previous measures. The multiple correlation between the independent variables—number of acts of racial violence, presence of literacy tests, presence of gubernatorial candidates favorable to Negroes, and presence of a bifactional Democratic party—and the dependent variable—Negro registration—is .345. The magnitude of this correlation seems to support previous findings. The political structure in the southern Negro's environment tends to place differential limits upon his opportunities for becoming registered. The next tests are to find the relationships between these aspects of the

---

[6] Donald R. Matthews and James W. Prothro, "Political Factors and Negro Voter Registration in the South," *American Political Science Review,* LVII (1963), 355–367.

political structure and activist norms, on the one hand, and between these aspects and Negro political involvement on the other hand. Table 5-2 shows these relationships.

TABLE 5-2
Relationships between Political Structure and Negro Political Involvement, and White Democratic Norms

	Agreement to Democratic Norms		Negro Political Involvement
	Activist	Popular	
Acts of Racial Violence	−.539	.057	−.051
Presence of Literacy Tests	−.335	.179	−.184
Presence of Favorable Gubernatorial Candidate	.281	−.021	.147
Presence of Bifactionalism	.261	−.042	.089

In Table 5-2 the effect of popular agreement to democratic norms is introduced as a comparison with the effect of activist agreement. The relationships between these two variables and the political structure variables contain higher levels of sampling error than does the relationship between political structure and Negro involvement. The reason for this is that activist norms, popular norms, and political structure are all measured at the aggregate level. The units of analysis for each correlation between these are the primary sampling unit rather than the individuals in the sample. Since there are obviously fewer sampling units than individuals, sampling error increases as these more aggregated variables are interrelated.

However, the fact that the relationships are consistent in all four political structure variables lends greater credence to these relationships. Thus activist agreement has a much greater effect across the board. This is also consistent with the finding that popular agreement has no direct effect on Negro registration. The reason that activist norms have the direct effect is that political practices restricting Negro registration are more likely to take place if activists, on the average, have low adherence to the value of Negro political equality. It should not be inferred that these practices are actually carried out by the activist stratum. In fact, some of these practices, such as acts of violence, may be more symptomatic of behavior among less active levels. To the extent that this is the case, we can conclude that activists tend to create an informal climate in which violence is viewed in varying degrees of respectability. This climate, then, may be supportive or nonsupportive of popular predispositions toward violence. It is the community climate that "triggers" predispositions, leading them to be translated into violence, discriminatory administrative action, and the like. Whatever the source of restrictive practices, they are more likely to take place if activist agreement is low, no matter what the level of popular agreement. Activist norms tend to account for those aspects of the political structure which relate differentially to Negro registration.

The relationships in Table 5-2 also show that the effects of political structure on Negro involvement are rather weak. Although we would normally expect to find a higher correlation when both variables are aggregate rather than individual measures, only in the case of literacy tests and favorable gubernatorial candidates is there any correlation at all. Those correlations support the conclusion drawn from Figure 5-2 that there tends to be some indirect effect from activist agreement to political involvement to Negro registration. One of the reasons that this indirect effect exists is that activist norms are related to the political structure, and that structure, in turn, has some effect on the Negro's psychological involvement. However, the primary inference that can be drawn from Table 5-2 concerns the secondary force of those linkages. The low correlations between political structure and Negro involvement underscore the possibility of a direct impact of political variables on Negro registration in the South.[7] The effect of political structure *in these data* is only secondarily due to its impact on involvement, being primarily independent of involvement. The restrictive nature of the local political system, therefore, may have important direct consequences for Negro registration.

---

[7] This finding is also consistent with the finding that these aggregate political variables affect Negro registration over and above the effect of aggregate social variables. See Matthews and Prothro, "Political Factors."

NEGRO SOCIAL STATUS AND
POLITICAL PARTICIPATION

The next attempt at elaboration will be to bring in "causes" of Negro political involvement which are alternatives to white activist attitudes so that the independent impact of activist attitudes can be sorted out. One of the most common assumptions about southern Negroes is that they have comparatively low social status; yet there may be a great deal of variation in Negro status throughout the South. In fact, Negro income, education, and occupational levels have been found to be a function of Negro density. Research constantly shows that individuals of lower social status have lower feelings of political involvement.[8] Negro density, then, might influence Negro registration; not only through the resulting restrictive sentiments among whites, but also through social status.

TABLE 5-3

Relationships between Negro Social Status, and Negro Proportion, Negro Political Involvement, and Negro Registration

	Negro Proportion	Negro Political Involvement	Negro Registration
Social Status Indicators			
Negro Income	−.350	.294	.369
Negro Education	−.243	.273	.262
Negro Occupation	−.270	.237	.207

Table 5-3 amasses some support for these hypotheses. Negro concentration has considerable effect on Negro social status. The correlations between Negro proportion and the social status indicators range from −.350 to −.270. These correlations indicate that there is also a correlation between lower Negro social status and high Negro density. In addition, a Negro's status effects his political involvement level. The correlations here range from .294 to .237. Likewise, higher social status brings a greater likelihood of a Negro's being registered. This relationship varies with the status

---

[8] See Lane, *Political Life.*

dimension, with the strongest correlation being .369 and the weakest, .207. In general, Negro concentration decreases Negro social status, which lowers political involvement and registration.

One of the interesting comparisons in Table 5-3 is between the correlations for involvement and registration. If the impact of involvement is wholly that of an intervening variable between registration and Negro social status, the correlations between status and involvement would be much higher than those between status and registration. This is not the case. The differences in the effects of status and involvement on registration vary with the status indicator. Moreover, the most important status indicator, income, has a greater correlation with registration than it does with involvement. This suggests two possibilities: Either involvement has a lesser impact on registration than does social status, or, as was hypothesized, the community context also competes independently with status and thus accounts for involvement. The first possibility can be tested by comparing the effect of status and involvement on registration. The correlation between involvement and registration was .544. However, the multiple correlation between all three status indicators and registration is .391. Involvement has a greater effect on whether or not a Negro will become registered; so the first possibility can be rejected. Therefore, both social status and white values may independently contribute to variation in Negro involvement.

If the Negro psychological state is not wholly independent of white attitudes, it is equally likely that Negro social status is also intertwined with white community sentiment. It is quite possible that the separation of the social status effect and the political effect is not as neat as the above paragraphs would indicate. The introduction to the model of the most important measure of Negro status gives the relationship suggested by Figure 5-3.

In Figure 5-3 the relationship between popular agreement and Negro income is not shown. That relationship, as the other effects of popular values, can be entirely explained by the relationship between popular and activist values on the one hand, and between activist agreement and Negro income on the other. The inference, then, is that the degree of democratic commitment at the popular level has no direct relationship to Negro income. Instead, the direct relationship, given this set of variables, is between activist attitudes and Negro income. In the case of this relationship, as with others in this analysis, a decision can be made between alternative dependencies. Negro income can be viewed as dependent upon white attitudes. One could construct theories incorporating, to some degree, the idea of Negro wealth as a cause of democratic attitudes among whites. The question of which causal pattern is correct is not important to the present analysis. Nevertheless, the other alternative possibilities are not as plausible as the alternative suggested by the model in Figure 5-3.

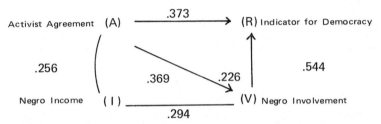

Figure 5-3. Relationship among Indicator for Democracy, Negro Income, Negro Political Involvement and Activist Agreement to Democratic Norms

The other relationships have been tested to evaluate whether, given the set of variables, they are direct effects. None can be rejected. Therefore, the appropriate inference is that all of these variables are interrelated. Although Negro income does have an important impact on Negro political involvement, this impact is not independent of the relationship between activist agreement and Negro income. In fact, the values of the correlations are quite close in magnitude. This means that any attempt at separating the impact of activist agreement on Negro involvement from the impact of Negro income would be of questionable validity.

Thus, the important point for this analysis is that Negro income and white attitudes (at least among the activists) are linked to one another. Therefore, just as it is not possible to talk about the separate effects of involvement and the community context on registration, so it is not possible to talk about the separate effects of Negro status and community sentiment on political involvement. These factors are intertwined as part of the same set of relationships that continue to be part of the legacy of southern history.

The interrelationship between activist attitudes and Negro income means that it is not possible to get valid estimates of their separate effects. Therefore, it may not be completely possible to think of the separate streams of relationships—some involving community effects and some involving psychological effects—on the dependent variable. A test of the extent to which the variables are intertwined in their effects on Negro registration is whether or not the theoretically proximate influences can explain the dependent variable as well as all influences combined.

Thus, if the social effect and a portion of the political effect occur through Negro involvement and, in addition, there is a direct political effect, then involvement and activist values should be explanatory of Negro registration. Moreover, these two variables should explain nearly as much of the dependent variable as all the less proximate variables put together. If we include the major variables discussed in this and previous chapters, we have a total of eight major independent variables in the study. These are: white activist agreement, white popular agreement, the Negro proportion, percent urban, percent of labor force in agriculture, percent of labor force in manufacturing, Negro income, and Negro political involvement. The multiple correlation between these eight independent variables and Negro registration is .66. On the other hand, only white activist agreement to democratic values and Negro political involvement can be treated as independent variables. The multiple correlation between these variables and Negro registration is .60. This indicates that the two variables can account for registration almost as well as can all eight. We can therefore conclude that the two proximate variables of involvement and white activist adherence to democratic norms go almost as far in explaining registration as do all major variables in this study put together.

On the other hand, Negro political involvement by itself produces a correlation of over .5. This single variable, therefore, does almost as well as the others combined; the eight variables explain about 15 percent more of the variance than political involvement alone, and the addition of activist attitudes to political involvement reduces the disparity by one-half. Activist values, therefore, have some impact over and above that of the Negro's psychological involvement. The eight variables together have some impact apart from activist attitudes and Negro involvement. Nevertheless, the central conclusion most in keeping with these data is that these variables form a cluster of interrelated effects.

The pattern may be a multicollinear one in which it is difficult to talk about the independent effects of each variable without
violating the assumptions underlying most routine analytical procedures.[9] Therefore, we may have two related streams of effects.
On the one hand, there seems to be a complex of factors associated
with the community—factors that affect the dependent variable
politically, psychologically, and socially. On the other hand, there
may be an additional impact from the political attitudes in the
community—attitudes associated with the prevailing political structure. Either way, the picture is essentially the same for the theoretical purposes at hand. It is not necessary to disregard or control
the effect of Negro psychological involvement to get an estimate
of how democratic the practices are in the South; the undemocratic
pattern is due, at least in part, to the low levels of Negro interest
in politics. It is not necessary to separate the effect of low social
status of Negroes to find the impact of the community context on
Negro involvement; low social status of Negroes is at least in part
concomitant with the differences in community contexts. In either
case, the community context remains either as a variable associated
with a complex pattern or as an important direct effect. In other
words, the individual attributes that have been measured go hand
in hand, to some extent, with the community context variables. To
the extent to which they do so, they spell out further meanings of
the community context for the individual Negroes who live in the
localities involved. One of the ways that blacks have been denied
political equality is through the denial of economic equality. In this
sense, the data quite accurately relate to us the patterns of democratic practice in the South. Similarly, where white activists disagree
with democratic values, Negroes are less apt to develop interest and
involvement in politics. The effect of the political structural variables means that it is possible that the objective factors in the
southern political world also affect Negro involvement. That is, the
social status of the individual Negro combines with the extent of
white restrictiveness in his community to affect his involvement. In
communities in which white norms on Negro political equality are
undemocratic, even Negroes of relatively high status may come

---

[9] For a discussion of the problems of multicollinearity see J.
Johnston, *Econometric Methods* (New York: McGraw-Hill, 1963),
pp. 201–207.

to feel that politics is outside their field of interest. If, historically, the values of the white majority have been restrictive toward Negro participation, the minority may not have developed the levels of interest and concern necessary for participation. Under these conditions, the political context of the southern region may affect Negro psychological orientations either more than, or in addition to, sociological factors.

CHAPTER SIX

Democratic Consensus and the Rules of the Game: A Causal Model

The empirical study of democratic practices has followed two broad trends. One emphasized the socio-economic factors which provide the conditions for the development of democratic rules of the game;[1] the other sought explanations of democracy primarily in the patterns of democratic consensus in political systems.[2] The latter stream of research indirectly provided the crucial hypotheses of this study—that citizen agreement to democratic values explains democratic practices. Thus, another way of talking about consensus is to talk about the attitudinal strain toward consensus in groups— or conformity. The fact that conformity to group norms takes place in human society means that democracy can never be fully

---

[1] See Seymour Martin Lipset, "Some Social Requisites of Democracy: Economic Development and Political Legitimacy," *American Political Science Review*, LIII (March 1959), 69–105; Phillips Cutright, "National Political Development," in Nelson Polsby, Robert A. Dentler, and Paul A. Smith, eds., *Politics and Social Life* (Boston: Houghton Mifflin, 1963), pp. 569–582; and Donald J. McCrone and Charles F. Cnudde, "Toward a Communications Theory of Democratic Political Development: A Causal Model," *American Political Science Review*, LXI (March 1967), 72–79.

[2] See James W. Prothro and Charles W. Grigg, "Fundamental Principles of Democracy: Bases of Agreement and Disagreement," *Journal of Politics*, XXII (1960), 276–294; Robert A. Dahl, *Who Governs?* (New Haven, Conn.: Yale University Press, 1961); and Herbert McClosky, "Consensus and Ideology in American Politics," *American Political Science Review*, LVIII (June 1964), 361–382.

achieved. However, the relative level of democracy will depend to some extent upon whether the community norm tends toward democratic or undemocratic directions. In this sense, the citizen attitudes toward democracy, in aggregate, serve as a context for the behaviors of the individuals in that context. If the behaviors have to do with democratic practices, citizen attitudes relate to democracy because of this contextual effect.

Since socio-economic variables can also be viewed as measures of the context for behavior, it is possible that social environment and democratic agreement variables are part of the same process. To date, no single study has tied these factors together into an explicit model of relationships. The present chapter attempts to do this by synthesizing the findings of the previous chapters.

In Chapter Two we explicated alternative conceptualizations of democracy. We settled upon the unidimensional definition of political equality as the dependent variable of the study. In that chapter we also developed the primary theory for explaining this variable: that of a relationship between aspects of the normative context and the rules of the game. In Chapter Three the social and historical setting of the South was briefly reviewed as the backdrop for the conduct of the tests. Out of that review we developed the operational definition of Negro registration for the dependent variable. We also developed there the most important social background factor in the contemporary South, Negro proportion in the local population. In the fourth and fifth chapters the influence of some aspects of the normative context was tested. We found differences in agreement to democratic values by levels of political activity. We tested the effect of inactivist and activist values on the dependent variable, and found activist values to be more important. In addition, there was an effect from the activist stratum which was mediated by the Negro's sense of involvement in political matters.

A MODEL OF DEMOCRACY

The analyses in these chapters generally suggest a pattern of relationships from social background factors to white activist and inactivist values to democratic practices. Moreover, in Chapter

Four we compared the multiple correlations involving all these variables to that correlation involving only the most proximate variables, activist agreement and Negro involvement. Given the assumption that activist agreement and Negro involvement are most proximate, the correspondence between the multiple correlations indicates that all the variables of the study form a developmental sequence. The effects of this sequence may be transmitted through the most proximate variables. This means that we may join all these variables into one empirical model of relationships that give rise to democracy in the South.

A rather complex system of relationships leads to what we have called the practice of democracy in the South. Yet these relationships can be represented quite adequately with a somewhat more parsimonious empirical model. This model begins with the social background of the individuals composing the region's white political majority. Included in this background are not only attributes such as economic status, but also the historical experiences of the communities in which whites reside. These factors give rise to values concerning political equality for Negroes. A separate consideration of activist and inactivist political strata indicates another factor relating to the democratic values of each stratum. Agreement to political equality among the activist stratum may influence popular agreement to that value. Alternatively, agreement to political equality among the popular stratum could also affect adherence to this value at the activist level. Finally, agreement to political equality among white activists affects Negro feelings toward political participation and Negro registration. These interlinked variables join in an empirical model leading to democracy in the South. Figure 6-1 illustrates this model.

Figure 6-1 represents a synthesis of the major propositions inferred from the analysis in the previous chapters. Taken together, these propositions are the most economic statement of the relationships which begin with Negro proportion and end with the indicator for democracy.

The model illustrates that there is a relationship between citizen attitudes and democratic practices. Although the consensus literature indicates that democracy can exist without a consensus on democratic values, this does not mean that the attitudes of the citizenry on democracy are unimportant for how democratic the system is. Moreover, as we would expect, if the citizens do have an impact on the rules of the game, the relationship increases with increases in political activity. The model illustrates that the attitudes of the activitists have the highest association with the dependent variable.

The model also illustrates the association between the attitudes of the two strata. The inference, therefore, is that the attitudes of the two sets of citizens probably do not differ markedly from each other as we move from one community to another. Further support for this inference is the fact that the attitudes of each are almost equally related to the social background and especially to Negro density in their immediate community context. Finally, it

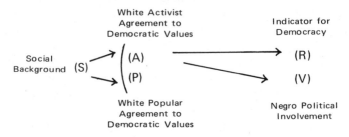

Figure 6-1. Model of Democracy in the South

appears that we cannot easily juxtapose the effect of the community context on Negro registration and the effect of the purely individual attributes of Negroes in order to estimate the contribution of each. The reason for this is that to some extent individual attributes such as political involvement, which may be related to political participation, are related to the community context variables. Rather than competing with the restrictiveness of the community, these factors help to spell out some of the intervening process through which the white community affects the rules of the game as far as Negroes are concerned.

The multiple correlation of .60, which was given in Chapter Four, shows the high degree of explanatory power of the model. This indicates that it goes much of the way toward explaining the variation in the practice of democracy in the South. Because of this level of economy and degree of explanation, the following pages will discuss the more general implications of the model.

IMPLICATIONS OF THE MODEL

It is possible to go beyond the model as a description of the pattern of relationships that exist in a cross-section of the South and even as a set of inferences about the process of democratic development. In other words, we can go beyond the data to guesses about what else might be true if these inferences are supported. In addition, there are some important normative issues that can be discussed as further implications of the model.

The pattern of the social, economic, and political forces in the South which are represented by the model seem to indicate that there would be little change in the patterns of Negro registration which would be generated by those aspects of the social context measured. When we move from a discussion of pure consensus on democratic values to one of more or less agreement on these values, we find that what the population thinks does have an impact on democratic practices. Moreover, that sector of the population most politically active has the greatest impact on the present practices.

However, the present practices include some relatively undemocratic patterns. The activist—the type of citizen that one would expect, *a priori,* to bring about innovation in a democratic direction—seems, according to the data, to be the one most responsible for the status quo. In addition, the attitudes of these citizens are as closely articulated with the usual indicator for the geographical distribution of the southern "way of life," Negro density, as are the attitudes of other citizens. The only deviation from this pattern is the additional impact that social status has upon the attitudes of the activist group.

Moreover, in many cases Negro psychological orientations toward politics seem to have developed in response to the prevailing political attitudes and practices in their communities and states. Therefore, great change in the political patterns cannot be expected to be derived from the activity of Negroes themselves, because where the situation is least democratic, the Negroes are least likely to be interested in politics. Part of the reason for this pattern may be that political and socio-economic features of Negro life are part of the same processes. Once again there may be a deviation from this pattern through the important impact of social status on Negro registration.

In short, the community context within which Negro behavior takes place in the South has important consequences. In the political arena, one important element in the community context is the level of agreement of the white population to democratic values. This community context may give rise to, or may be part of, the same complex of factors with the purely individual characteristics of Negroes.

This inference suggests an informal mechanism of activist control over the rules of the game. The most direct method for eliminating undemocratic practices would be the development of protest activity by the group that is denied political equality. However, our data indicate that, among the stratum, the undemocratic values that affect democratic practices also lessen the possibility that such protest activity will take place. Interest and concern for politics generally would be necessary for individuals to become aroused about their lack of access to politics. If such involvement is a precondition of protest, however, then protest is least likely to take place where the rules of the game are most restrictive. Thus, undemocratic practices are partially accounted for by low levels of Negro involvement in politics. Undemocratic values among white activists account, in part, for low levels of Negro involvement. Therefore, the psychological reactions among the minority that is denied political equality tend to reinforce the activist stratum's ability to influence the rules of the game.

These comments suggest that contemporary Negro protest activity occurred in the least restrictive areas of the South. In those areas, white activists are more likely to agree to democratic values. Where this agreement takes place, Negroes are more likely to have developed the involvement that would lead them to participate in protest activity. Certainly the early Negro demonstrations indicate that this might be the case: those demonstrations were concentrated in the urban areas of the region. In those areas social status, economic change, and historical effects are least likely to work against democratic agreement.

The model also suggests a direct effect from activist agreement to democratic practices. Thus higher levels of activist agreement go hand-in-hand with higher levels of political equality for Negroes. Yet political systems may operate with highly democratic rules of the game even if there is a dissensus on democratic values in the population. Under those conditions, the rules of the game would simply be less democratic than a corresponding system in which there is greater democratic agreement.

The implication of this conclusion is that there are additional variables that can help determine how democratic a system is. How much democracy we would have, given a certain level of democratic agreement—a level approaching a consensus, for example—cannot be estimated accurately until the effects of other variables have been taken into consideration. In this study, democratic agreement has been found to be an important variable; however, the level of explanation cannot, by any stretch of the imagination, support unicausal statements.

An additional implication is that there may be some effect of popular attitudes on the attitudes of the activists. There was some relationship between the attitudes of the two strata. One possible reason for the relationship is that the activists influence what others in their locality think. However, the level of activist agreement may depend, to a certain extent, upon the values of the inactivists. We can understand how such a pattern of causality might come about, even though there does not appear to be a developmental sequence from popular attitudes to activist attitudes to the rules of the game. That understanding depends upon a conceptual comparison between the activist role and that of an ideal type, the organizational leader.

Theoretically, there can be two general categories of pressures on leadership.[3] One arises from the internal demands of the organization. These pressures have to do with motivations of the lower echelons to maintain the existing sub-organization structures. Another pressure on leadership emanates from outside the organization. These external pressures result from the leadership's desire to sustain the organization through adapting it to environmental change. When these external and internal pressures are in conflict, "responsible" leadership must react to both pressures, attempting to adjust their effects. As a result, intra-organization conflict is reduced while points of view supporting one or the other source of pressure are incompletely satisfied.

---

[3] Philip Selznick, *Leadership in Administration* (Evanston, Ill.: Row, Peterson, 1957).

> This problem of accommodating internal and ex-
> ternal demands is a source of much misunderstanding.
> It divides administrative analysts and responsible officials
> into hostile camps. The leader, sensitive to internal
> pressures and to the heavy price that must be paid for
> co-operation, is impatient with the analyst whose narrow
> logic of efficiency leads to proposals for change that are
> irresponsible from the stand-point of the institution.[4]

The underlying dimension that divides leaders from others
and that leads to accommodating behavior seems to be one of a
sense of responsibility. The leaders, in their role as leaders, tend
to feel a greater degree of responsibility for the future of the organization; therefore, they try to take into consideration the demands
of those who hold other roles in the organization, as well as the
pressures from the environment. When the pressures from within
the organization conflict with the needs of the organization to
adjust to the environment, those making the internal demands are
often said to be irresponsible. Yet it is normally the leader of the
organization who, in effect, assigns weights to these conflicting
pressures, or otherwise accommodates them.

The assumption, then, of applying this analogy to the data
on activists and inactivists is not that the former are leaders; it is
clear that, except for a very few, they are not. The assumption
is that the activists feel a greater sense of responsibility for the
future of the community, region, way of life, etc. Therefore, if the
activists feel greater responsibility than the inactivists, the analogy
may apply to a certain extent even though they are not leaders
and do not have the even greater sense of responsibility of persons
in that role. This assumption seems to be not unrealistic, given
the data in the United States on the association between attitudes
such as sense of civic duty and political activity.

The analogy helps in understanding these findings. These
data indicate that the more politically active strata, simply because
of their higher activity, have a greater direct impact on the nature
of the local political system. Since they are closer to the level of
the actual decision-makers, the activists are more likely to help
shape the decision-making mechanism. However, this shaping does
not occur in a vacuum. Several factors—which may be termed

---

[4] *Ibid.,* pp. 73–74.

internal and external considerations—may be engaged in making decisions about the nature of the rules of the game.

Among the factors that could be included in any change in the rules of the game are popular values. Any change that violates the inactivists' values may be countered by a more active populace. This sequence of events rarely occurs because the upper stratum tends to defer to the inactivists' wishes. One aspect of the activist role, therefore, is that of evaluating the desires of the less active, yet potentially involved, sectors of the community. Through this kind of "rule of anticipated reactions," popular values within the community would be, in effect, consulted by the activists.[5] Therefore, the inactivists could achieve some degree of representation of their values among the upper stratum.

On the other hand, activists must frequently take values outside the community into consideration. The historical setting of the South brings two factors to mind here. First, the further industrialization of the region means that communities that aspire to industrialization must negotiate increasingly with outside capital. The history of political inequality for Negroes runs counter to the rest of the nation's democratic public ideology. Therefore, community activists who want to attract industry may feel a need to conform to the general public ideology.[6] Our data from Chapter Three indicate that, as dependence on agriculture decreases, political equality for Negroes increases. Secondly, the more highly educated and less provincial members of the activist stratum may be sincerely concerned with the discrepancy between the national ideology and the political practices in the South. Our data from Chapter Four indicate that social status brings higher levels of democratic agreement among the activists than it does among the inactivists. An external orientation, as another aspect of the leadership role, therefore might lead to change in the rules of the game in a more democratic direction. At the same time, this aspect of the role might lead to attempts at the implementation of structures to maintain democracy. An example of such a structure would

---

[5] For the latest formulation of this rule, see Carl J. Friedrich, *Man and His Government* (New York: McGraw-Hill, 1963), pp. 199–215.

[6] An additional factor here may be the threat of social unrest that the conflict between the public ideology and political reality elicits from Negroes in restrictive communities.

be civic training in the schools to increase the inactivists' commitment to democratic values. Another example would be the informal creation of a climate of respectability for articulation of values that approximate those of the activists.

Consideration of a more complex theory of activist roles thus suggests that the more active stratum mediates between intra-community and extra-community factors. This mediation brings about gradual adjustments in the rules of the game. An implication of the model is that the changes in the degree of democratic practices throughout the region occurred through these interactions. The picture that this possibility indicates, however, is one of evolutionary rather than revolutionary change.

The general implication is that for the era prior to the civil rights revolution, which is when these data were gathered, change in the rules of the game was primarily due to external forces. The model suggests that the source of internal strain, Negro predispositions to participate, would produce only marginal degrees of change because such attitudes were meager where the rules of the game were most restrictive. On the other hand, it is possible that the wider American value system influenced the rules of the game in southern communities. This may have occurred if the activists behaved in accommodating ways, giving both the wider value system and the local one influence on political practices.

In more recent years, it is quite possible that the pattern has changed considerably in the South. The election of black mayors and other officials in Mississippi may mean that the model and implications that have been drawn from it are no longer descriptive of the region. Changes could have developed out of purely internal conflicts, in this case, conflicts emanating from the black community. Therefore, it would be improper to conclude that the conclusions that have been drawn mean that internally generated change is never possible. The conclusion, rather, is that internally generated change was highly improbable at the time the data were collected.

The suggestion that black activism led to internally generated change points out that present developments also may provide "natural experiments" for testing additional, even more interesting, hypotheses and theories. Measures of the differences in Negro participation throughout the South, prior to the increase in democratic practices, were necessary for answers to the theoretical questions at issue in this book. The hope that these differences will no longer exist does not invalidate these tests, but points to the opportunity for different tests.

Nevertheless, the analogy drawn to account for the patterns present in these data presents a picture of the more politically active citizens as conservatives. They are conservative in the sense that they are likely to feel "responsible" for preserving the social order.[7] Therefore, they may try somehow to accommodate discontinuities and strains between various values that underlie that order. In the South, these strains are between the local view of Negro participation and the American creed of equality.

Of course, as we move up the ladder of political stratification, we would probably find political leaders with an even greater sense of responsibility on these dimensions. There we would expect the pattern to be similar to that spelled out here, but to a greater extreme. There seems to be a sizeable portion of the citizenry who have attitudes on Negro participation which are in concert with the ability of Negroes to register to vote in their locality. By inference, we have concluded that this portion of the citizenry has an impact on the practice of democracy in their communities. Our guess is that they have this impact because they play a role, not only as "carriers of the creed," but also as "accommodators of the creed." As such, they may play intermediary parts in conflicts between the American value system and the development of greater political equality in the South.

In conclusion, we can say that if conformity is usually found in human groups, then perhaps the best we can hope for in establishing democratic practices is to bring about a particular kind of conformity—conformity to democratic norms. The development of such conformity may require that individuals with non-democratic attitudes be discriminated against in informal social relations. As a result, this conformity would lead to less freedom of discussion than that posited by the ideal of democracy—complete tolerance for even undemocratic opinions. However, given the fragile nature of political opinions, especially of tolerance itself, perhaps the only

---

[7] The findings showing the overwhelming support of the traditional American values among political activists would also lead to this conclusion. For a summary see Lester W. Milbrath, *Political Participation* (Chicago: Rand McNally, 1965), pp. 142–154.

way to bring about any level of democracy at all is to do it through an informal reign of intolerance for intolerance. My guess is that, in the South, conformity to the national, rather than to the regional values, goes hand in hand with greater democracy because the former values are more democratic.

I should hasten to say that I am talking about informal norms and not about the law. Formal rules restricting undemocratic behaviors could be applied to democratic behaviors with simply a change in the personnel or in the attitudes of the personnel in the enforcing agencies. However, conformity as an informal rule of behavior already restricts the freedom to arrive at individual political decisions. So the most democratic effect possible, given that circumstance, seems to be to turn the restriction against behaviors that are undemocratic. In that way at least the community or system is protected from the dangers of a development of conformity to undemocratic practices.

Real political systems probably contain norms of conformity to practices that are democratic in some respects and undemocratic in others. How secure democracy is, then, depends upon the overall effect of these norms taken together. Some areas in the South contain norms democratic as far as one type of practice is concerned—Negro political participation. One of the reasons that this occurs is that the more politically active whites, who have become socialized to believe in democratic norms, have a greater effect on what happens to Negroes in those areas. However, there is no basis for the belief that democratic systems are protected against undemocratic threats merely because of the values of the active groups. If the values of the activists explain political patterns where those patterns are democratic, they explain the patterns just as well where they are undemocratic. Because activists have a greater impact upon the system, they are responsible for the undemocratic as well as the democratic features of the South. Therefore, the examination of the southern "deviant case" indicates that dependence upon activists to maintain democratic practices is not a very secure state of affairs. External pressures such as the occurrence of economic crises, war, or internal violence, could produce modifications in activist norms leading to new, perhaps even more undemocratic, patterns of conformity.

Appendix

There are some methodological issues raised by this analysis that should be discussed. The most common one is disagreement over whether or not one should use product-moment correlation with survey data. Although such usage has had a long history in the voting studies, statistical purists charge that the measure assumes that survey data are not (or more properly, are rarely thought of as) interval data.

This charge is not applicable to most of the independent variables used in this book. They are what are normally considered interval measures. Exceptions are: Negro education, which is a ranking dependent upon number of years of education completed; Negro occupation, which is a ranking by judges of occupational categories along an occupational prestige dimension; and Negro political involvement, which is a simple cumulative index. The first two variables above do not figure prominently in the book. Involvement does, but its correlation with the dependent variable is the highest in the book and is among the highest reported between two variables measured at the individual level. I assume that if there is any error in treating involvement as an interval measure, it is not in the direction of understating its effect on the dependent variable. Since this effect is primarily one that competes with the main hypothesis, this assumption means that the procedure is a conservative one.

The other independent variables are either proportions or medians obtained from the U.S. Census, or proportions that are either computed from the survey materials or measured as other units, such as Negro income, which is measured in hundreds of dollars. There seems to be agreement that these measures are interval scales. Besides Negro political involvement, the only problem of this nature concerns the dependent variables. These are behaviors that have either been engaged in or not, or are answers to attitude items that the respondent can either agree to or not. In both cases these dichotomous items have been treated as interval measures, scored either "0" or "1." Therefore the nature of the dependent variables is such that, by definition, most would consider them to be interval measures.

But this raises another, more interesting, issue. Normally, in relationships in which one variable is a dichotomous measure, we can expect a threshold effect at the lower end of the curve and a ceiling effect at the top. This raises the possibility that the relationships may be only approximately linear and that the disturbance term may be proportional to the independent variable, thus violating the assumption of homoscedasticity. In this case, the estimates of the constants of proportionality will be inefficient.

However, the advantages of more accurate estimates do not seem to justify the complications of transformation, or the use of statistical measures that are less understood than conventional correlation. If the analysis had been other than an inspection for variables related to the dependent variable, that is, if we had theories that specified constants of proportionality of certain magnitudes, or if accurate estimates of those constants had been crucial to the theory, then these other procedures would have been relied upon in the body of the book.[1]

Another matter that might concern some readers is the absence of tests of significance. Since the dependent variables are individual-based measures that have been gathered through surveys, the size of the samples are large enough to produce statistical significance where any relationship worth mentioning exists. The exceptions to this rule are not given much weight in the analysis and are called to the attention of the reader in the body of the discussion, where all statements dealing with such relationships are properly qualified. Yet all this merely serves to demonstrate a problem with conventional tests of significance when survey data are used. Few surveys are conducted with sample sizes so small that relationships will not reach significance. Yet we often see scholars in these cases reporting significance tests as if there were doubt as to the outcome. Although there has been some con-

---

[1] A check was made using probit analysis, a procedure designed for dichotomous dependent variables. The coefficients obtained from that test have the same rank order as the statistically significant coefficients in Tables A-1 and A-2 below. For a discussion of probit analysis see Arthur S. Goldberger, *Econometric Theory* (New York: Wiley & Sons, 1964), pp. 250–251.

troversy surrounding tests of significance, that controversy has not yet shed light on this aspect of the problem.

Finally, the actual variables used were taken from the 1960 U.S. Census for the counties included in the sample and from the Negro Political Participation Study, Institute for Research in Social Science, University of North Carolina, Chapel Hill, North Carolina. The census variables were not modified in any way and were simply conceptualized as contextual attributes of the individuals who were in the sample who lived in the corresponding county. Few of the survey variables were transformed; the exceptions are given and described in the above discussion or in the body of the book. The survey data are available through the Inter-University Consortium for Political Research, Ann Arbor, Michigan.

The items used in the Negro Political Involvement index were not described fully elsewhere. They are:

1. "Generally speaking, how interested are you in politics—a great deal, somewhat, or not at all?"
2. "Generally speaking, do you usually think of yourself as a Republican, a Democrat, an Independent, or what?"
If "Democrat": "Would you call yourself a strong Democrat or a not very strong Democrat?"
If "Republican": "Would you call yourself a strong Republican or a not very strong Republican?"
If "Independent," "Other," "Don't Know": Do you think of yourself as closer to the Republican or Democratic party?"
(The party identification index is created out of these items. It runs from strong Democrat to strong Republican. It is then folded to give strength of identification rather than partisan direction.)
3. "There's not much use in people like me voting because all of the candidates are usually against what I want."

The index was constructed according to Guttman scaling procedures; items with more than dichotomous responses were dichotomized in whichever way minimized errors, but errors were not so reassigned.

Finally, Tables A-1 and A-2 give tests of significance of the estimates and of the regression coefficients corresponding to the equation

$$Ym = Xbm + Vm$$

where Ym is a $T \times 1$ vector of observations on the dependent variable, X is the $T \times X$ matrix of observations on all independent variables, bm is the $K \times 1$ vector of coefficients and Vm is the $T \times 1$ vector of disturbances assumed to be uncorrelated with any independent variable.

TABLE A-1

Regression Coefficients and Tests of Significance between Independent Variables and the Dependent Variable, Negro Registration

Variables in the Equation	Value of Coefficient	Significance Level
Activist Attitudes	.00075	P < .001
Inactivist Attitudes	−.00035	.05 > P > .001
Negro Involvement	.15399	P < .001

In Table A-1 all independent variables reach some acceptable level of significance. However, the coefficient for inactivist values is half that of activist values, conforming to the conclusions drawn in the body of the book.[2] Moreover, the sign of this coefficient is negative, further underscoring the observation that the measure of popular attitudes has a probable spurious or a possible negative relationship with the dependent variable. Table A-2 gives the same

---

[2] The large differences between the coefficients for Negro Involvement and activist attitudes are in part due to the differences in scale in the measures of the variables. The Beta weights (which are standardized to take these differences into account) for the variables are:

Negro Involvement:	.4866
Activist Attitudes:	.3179
Inactivist Attitudes:	−.1079

Parameter estimates from two-stage least squares conform to the ranking of these Beta weights and the ordinary least square estimates. In the two-stage least squares tests the assumption about the disturbances was relaxed, allowing for the possibility of reciprocal relationships between activist and inactivist attitudes, by selectively bringing into the matrix enough "exogenous" variables to achieve "over-identification." See J. Johnston, *Econometric Methods* (New York: McGraw-Hill, 1960), pp. 236–237 and 258–260.

coefficients after the more important census variables are added to the equation.

TABLE A-2

Regression Coefficients and Tests of Significance among Independent Variables and the Dependent Variable with Census Variables Added

Variables in the Equation	Value of Coefficient	Significance Level
Activist Attitudes	.00074	$P < .001$
Inactivist Attitudes	.00055	$P < .001$
Negro Involvement	.13304	$P < .001$
Negro Proportion	.00021	$P > .05$
Urban Proportion	.00012	$P > .05$
Proportion in Agricultural Occupations	.00083	$P < .001$
Proportion in Manufacturing Occupations	.00029	$P > .05$

Table A-2 shows that the addition of these other community background characteristics to the equation does not markedly change the values of the coefficients except for that corresponding to the effect of popular attitudes. This once again supports the conclusions drawn from the correlational analysis. Moreover, only one of the census variables is significant when activist attitudes and Negro involvement are in the equation. This evidence is consistent with the conclusion that these variables are part of the same stream of effects and cannot be easily separated.

Index